THE PRINCIPLES OF HORSEMANSHIP

BY

F. BAUCHER

TRANSLATED FROM THE FRENCH

BY

JOHN SWIRE

British Library Cataloguing-in-Publication Data
A catalogue record for this book is available from the
British Library

Contents

Horses – Sports and Utility

The horse (Equus ferus caballus) is one of two extant subspecies of Equus ferus. It is an odd-toed ungulate mammal belonging to the taxonomic family 'Equidae'. The horse has evolved over the past 45 to 55 million years from a small multi-toed creature into the large, single-toed animal of today. Humans began to domesticate horses around 4000 BC, and their domestication is believed to have been widespread by 3000 BC. We, as humans have interacted with horses in a multitude of ways throughout history – from sport competitions and non-competitive recreational pursuits, to working activities such as police work, agriculture, entertainment and therapy. Horses have also been used in warfare, from which a wide variety of riding and driving techniques developed, using many different styles of equipment and methods of control. With this range of uses in mind, there is an equally extensive, specialized vocabulary used to describe equine-related concepts, covering everything from anatomy to life stages, size, colours, markings, breeds, locomotion, and behaviour.

Sporting events are some of the largest and best-known activities involving horses, and here – communication between human and horse is paramount. To aid this process, horses are usually ridden with a saddle on their backs to assist the rider with balance and positioning, and a bridle or related headgear to assist the rider in maintaining control. Historically, equestrians honed their craft through games and races; providing skills needed for battle, as well as entertainment for home crowds. Today, these competitions have evolved into racing, dressage, eventing and show jumping – many of which have their origins in military training, focused on control and balance of both the horse and rider. Other sports, such as rodeo, developed from practical skills such as those needed on working ranches and stations. Horse racing of all types evolved from impromptu competitions between riders or drivers, and has since become a multi-million pound industry. It is watched in almost every nation of the world, in its three main forms: 'flat racing' (long, even stretches), 'steeplechasing' (racing over jumps) and 'harness racing' (where horses trot or pace whilst pulling a driver in a small, light cart). A major part of horse racing's economic importance lies in the gambling associated with it.

All forms of competition, requiring demanding and specialized skills from both horse and rider, resulted in the systematic development of specialized breeds and equipment for each sport. Horse shows, which have their origins in medieval European fairs, are held around the world. They host a huge range of classes, covering all of the mounted and harness disciplines, as well as 'In-hand' classes where the horses are led, rather than ridden, to be evaluated on their conformation. The method of judging varies with the discipline, but winning usually depends on style and ability of both horse and rider. Sports such as polo do not judge the horse itself, but rather use the horse as a partner for human competitors as a necessary part of the game. Although the horse requires specialized training to participate, the details of its performance are not judged, only the result of the rider's actions—be it getting a ball through a goal or some other task. A similar, historical example of sports partnerships between human and horse is 'jousting', in which the main goal is for one rider to unseat the other. This pastime is still practiced by some sportsmen today.

There are certain jobs that horses do very well, and no technology has yet developed to fully replace them. For example, mounted police horses are still effective for certain types of patrol duties and crowd control. Cattle ranches still require riders on horseback to round up cattle that are scattered across remote, rugged terrain. In more urban areas, horses used to be the main form of transport, in the form of pulling carriages, and are still extensively used (especially in the UK) for ceremonial functions, i.e. horse-drawn carriages transporting dignitaries, military personnel or even the royal family. Horses can also be used in areas where it is necessary to avoid vehicular disruption to delicate soil, such as nature reserves. They may also be the only form of transport allowed in wilderness areas, often because of the fact that horses are quieter than motorised vehicles, therefore impacting less on their surroundings. Although machinery has replaced horses in many parts of the world, an estimated 100 million horses, donkeys and mules are still used for agriculture and transportation in less developed areas. This number includes around 27 million working animals in Africa alone.

As well as these labour intensive uses, horses can also be incredibly valuable for therapy. People of all ages with physical and mental disabilities obtain beneficial results from association with horses. Therapeutic riding is used to mentally and physically stimulate disabled persons and help them improve their lives through improved balance and coordination, increased self-confidence, and a greater feeling of freedom and independence. Horses also provide psychological benefits to people whether they actually ride or not. 'Equine-assisted' or 'equine-facilitated' therapy is a form of experiential psychotherapy that uses horses as companion animals to assist people with mental illness, including anxiety disorders, psychotic disorders, mood disorders, behavioural difficulties, and those who are going through major life changes. There are also experimental programs using horses in prison settings. Exposure to horses appears to improve the behaviour of inmates and help reduce recidivism when they leave.

As a concluding note, one of the most important aspects of equine care is farriery; a specialist in equine hoof care. Horses aid humans in so many ways, it is important to ensure that they are properly equipped and cared for. Farriers have largely replaced blacksmiths (after this specialism mostly became redundant after the industrial revolution), and are highly skilled in both metalwork and horse anatomy. Historically, the jobs of farrier and blacksmith were practically synonymous, shown by the etymology of the word: farrier comes from Middle French ferrier (blacksmith), and from the Latin word ferrum (iron). Modern day farriers usually specialize in horseshoeing though, focusing their time and effort on the care of the horse's hoof, including trimming and balancing of the hoof, as well as the placing of the shoes. Additional tasks for the farrier include dealing with injured or diseased hooves and application of special shoes for racing, training or 'cosmetic' purposes. In countries such as the United Kingdom, it is illegal for people other than registered farriers to call themselves a farrier or to carry out any farriery work, the primary aim being 'to prevent and avoid suffering by and cruelty to horses arising from the shoeing of horses by unskilled persons.' This is not the case in all countries however, where horse protection is severely lacking.

We hope the reader enjoys this book.

PREFACE

Having a well-founded belief in the method of horse training originated by Mons. F. Baucher, I have had pleasure in translating the 10th Edition of his book, which was written before he developed the theory that the legs and hands should act separately, instead of mutually assisting one another. His method is simple and practical; he treats a horse like a human being; he maintains that the rider can only influence his mount by placing it in such a position that the movement desired is the only possible one, and then stimulating it; the placing being made easy by specially graduated exercises which supple the horse's will as well as his muscles. The Author also gives instructions as to how to obtain the balance which will enable the horse to work with the least strain to the various parts of the body, and so prolong the period of its usefulness.

Mons. Baucher lived in the reigns of Louis Philippe and Napoleon III.; he was not only a skilled horseman and horsemaster, thoroughly conversant with all the secrets of his art, but he proved the excellence of his methods by training horses to the height of perfection and showing them in public.

I recommend that this book should be used as an introduction to "Cavalry Horsemanship and Horse Training," by Lt.-Col. Blacque Belair, and to "Riding and Breaking," by James Fillis.

J. SWIRE.

1918.

M. BAUCHER

THE PRINCIPLES OF HORSEMANSHIP

CHAPTER I

NEW METHOD OF GIVING THE RIDER A GOOD SEAT

The reader will no doubt wonder why, in the earlier editions of this work dealing with the training of the horse, I did not commence by explaining the position of the rider, a part of horsemanship which has always had such prominence in classical writings.

I have, however, had a good reason for putting off till now discussing this question. If I had not anything new to say, I could, in the usual way, have consulted the works of my predecessors, and after transposing a few phrases and changing a few words, launched on the equestrian world one more useless book. But I had other ideas; I wished to introduce something quite new. My system of giving a good position to the rider being also an innovation, I feared that too many new instructions would terrify the amateurs, and even those with the best intentions would put me at the mercy of my opponents, who would not fail to proclaim that my means of influencing the horse were impracticable, or that they could not be applied except with the help of a position still more impracticable. Now, I have proved the contrary: under my system horses have been trained by the troop, no matter what the position of the men may have been. To give more weight to this method, to make it more clearly understood, I had at first to detach it from other minor matters, and keep silence about the new principles which concerned the position of the rider: I therefore waited the complete success of the official experiments before putting them forward. By means of these principles, added to those which I have published connected with the training of horses, I equally shorten the training of the man, and I establish a precise and complete system for each of these two important parts of horsemanship which have so far been treated as one.

By following my new directions with regard to the position of the rider a prompt and certain result will be attained, whilst they are as easy to understand as to explain. Two sentences are sufficient to explain everything to the rider. It is of the greatest importance, so far as the understanding and progress of the pupil is concerned, that the instructor should be concise, clear and persuasive; he should, therefore, avoid overwhelming his recruits by long drawn-out theoretical explanations. A few well-chosen words, spoken at the right time, will appeal much more quickly to the understanding. Silent observation is often one of the distinctive characteristics of a good instructor. When once the principle laid down has been thoroughly understood the instructor should leave a studious pupil to work it out for himself; it is only in this way that he will succeed in discovering the effects of tact which cannot be obtained except by practice.

Position of the rider.—The rider should sit as upright as possible, so that each part of his body rests on that which is immediately below it, and produces direct vertical pressure through the seat bones; the arms should hang easily along the sides; the thighs and the legs should, with their inward sides, take as many points of contact as possible with the saddle and the sides of the horse; the feet will follow naturally the movements of the legs.

One understands from these few lines how very simple the position of the rider is.

The means which I recommend for obtaining a good position in a short time, remove all the difficulties associated with the methods laid down by my predecessors. The pupil hardly understood anything of the long catechism, loudly recited by the instructor, from the first to the last sentence; and in consequence he could not carry out his directions. Here one word takes the place of all these sentences, after the pupil has passed through a course of suppling exercises. This work will make the rider active and intelligent, and a month will not have passed before the heaviest and most awkward conscript will have attained a really good seat.

Preparatory lesson. (Lessons should last an hour, and there should be two lessons each day for a month.)

The horse is brought out saddled and bridled; the instructor should have not less than two pupils; one pupil will hold the horse by the bridle, and closely observe the work of the other, so as to learn what to do in his turn. The other pupil should stand by the horse's shoulder and prepare to mount; he should take hold of the mane with the right hand and pass it into the left hand, which should hold it as near the roots as possible without twisting the hair; he should next take hold of the pommel of the saddle with the four fingers of the right hand; then, after bending the knees slightly, he should raise himself with his hands, and when his waist is level with the withers, pass the right leg over the back without touching it, and place himself lightly in the saddle. This vaulting movement being of great service in developing the agility of the rider, the instructor should make the pupil repeat it several times before allowing him to seat himself in the saddle, and before long the repetition of this exercise will give him the measure of what he can do with the power he has in his arms and loins.

Work in the saddle.—(This work should be done with the horse standing; the horse should be preferably old and quiet. The reins should be knotted and allowed to fall on the neck.) When the pupil has mounted the horse the instructor should consider his natural position, and make note of the parts which require the most. frequent exercise owing to their tendency to slackness or stiffness.

The instructor will commence the lesson by giving his attention to the upper part of the pupil's body. In order to press back the shoulders he should tell his pupil to hollow his back and press his waist forward; and in the case of a man with slack loins keep him in this position for some time without considering the stiffness which it will cause at first. It is by acting energetically that the pupil will become supple, and not by taking the easy position so often and so wrongly recommended. A movement at first obtained with great effort will become easy in a short time, because of the skill which it develops, and because in this case skill is merely the result of the appropriate combination and employment of the muscles. That which the pupil at first succeeded in doing by the expenditure of 20 lbs. of force, will soon only require 14 lbs., then 10 lbs., and then 4 lbs. Skill requires only the expenditure of 4 lbs. of force.

If one were to commence with a small amount of effort this result could not be attained. The pupil should, therefore, frequently repeat the bending in of the waist, whilst occasionally allowing himself to return to his naturally relaxed state, in order that he may thoroughly understand how to employ his strength so as to quickly give his body a good position. The body being well placed the instructor passes to (1) the exercise for the arm, which consists in moving it in every direction, first bent and then straight; (2) the exercise for the head, which should be turned to the right and left without the movement affecting the shoulders.

When the lessons given to the body, the arms, and the head have had a satisfactory result, which should be attained in four days (eight lessons), the instructor will commence the exercise for the legs.

The pupil should remove one of his thighs as far from the saddle as possible, and then bring it back again with an inward rotary movement, so that it feels the saddle with as many points of contact as possible, the instructor taking care that the thigh does not fall back heavily into its place: it should retake its position with a slow progressive movement and gently. He should, in fact, during the first lesson, take the pupil's leg and direct its movement, so as to clearly explain the manner in which the displacement should be made. He will thus avoid tiring his pupil and will obtain good results more promptly.

This kind of exercise is very tiring at first, and requires frequent periods of rest, and no good will be obtained by prolonging the duration of the work beyond the capabilities of the pupil. The movements which bring the thigh near the saddle, and those that take it away from it having become more easy, the thighs will have acquired a suppleness which will enable them to take a good position in the saddle. The instructor will then commence the exercises for the legs.

The bending of the legs.—The instructor should see that the knees always remain close to the saddle. The legs will move backwards and forwards like the pendulum of a clock, that is the pupil will bend the knees until the heels touch the back of the saddle. By repeating these bending exercises the legs will soon become supple, pliant and independent of the thighs. These bending exercises of the legs and thighs should be continued for four days (eight lessons). In order to make each of these movements more correct and easy, eight days should be devoted to them. The fourteen days which remain to complete the month will be given up to suppling exercises in a stationary position; to teach the pupil to combine the power of his arms with that of his loins the instructor will give him weights, varying from ten to twenty pounds progressively, to hold with the arms stretched upwards. He will commence this exercise in the position which is the least tiring, the arm being bent and the hand near the shoulder, the hand should then be pressed gradually upwards to the full extent of the arm. The body should not be influenced by this movement, but should remain in the same position.

The knees.—The pressing power of the knees can be arrived at, and developed by the following means, which, though at first may perhaps seem futile, will nevertheless soon bring very great results. The instructor will get a piece

15

of leather of suitable thickness and length, say, a quarter of an inch thick and two feet long, and will place one end between the knee and the saddle. The pupil should use all the force of his knee pressure to prevent the instructor from pulling the leather away with gradually increasing force. By this means the instructor will be able to measure the increasing strength of his pupils, and he should encourage each one of them at the right time with a word of praise. The instructor must take the greatest care when exercising separately any one part of the body that other parts are not put into movement, as for example the movement of the arm should not affect the shoulder; the same with the thighs and the body, and the legs and the thighs. The displacement and suppling of each isolated part once obtained, the instructor will cause the pupil to momentarily displace the body and seat so as to teach him to get back into the saddle without assistance. This exercise is carried out in the following way. The instructor, standing beside the horse, should push the pupil's hip until his seat is beyond the saddle. Before displacing his pupil again the instructor will allow him to get back into the saddle, taking care that to regain his seat he only vises his hips and knees, that is to say the parts nearest the seat. In fact help from the shoulders will soon have effect upon the hands, and these on the horse, and help from the legs would produce still greater inconvenience. In a word, in all the displacements the instructor must impress on the pupil never to use in directing the horse the force which keeps him in the saddle, and, vice versa, not to use to keep himself in the saddle the parts with which he controls his horse.

The pupil, having passed through the preliminary ordeals, will await with impatience the first movements of the horse, in order to adapt himself to them with the ease of an experienced horseman.

Fifteen days (thirty lessons) should be given up to the walk, the trot, and even the canter. The pupil should give his whole attention to following the movements of the horse, and, in consequence, the instructor will sec that he takes pains in keeping his position right, without thinking of guiding his horse. The rider should only be asked to walk straight forward, and then in every direction, with a bridoon rein held in each hand. At the end of four days (eight lessons) he can be allowed to hold all the reins in the left hand. The instructor will see that the right hand is placed by the side of the left hand, in order that the rider may, at an early date, form the habit of sitting square in the saddle with the shoulders in line. The horse should trot both to the right and left. When the seat has been made firm at all the paces, the instructor should explain in simple language the relation which ought to exist between the hands and the legs, as well as their separate effects.

The Education of the horse.—The rider should now commence the education of the horse by following the progression which I have explained in previous editions and which will be again found in what follows. The instructor will explain to the pupil the close connection that exists between the education of the man and that of the horse. It will not be more than four months before the recruit can be passed on to the training in company; the words of command will now be only an affair of memory, and on hearing them he will carry them out, because he will be master of his horse.

I hope the cavalry will understand (as it has already appreciated my method of educating the horse) the full advantage to be obtained from the means which I have explained for making the very best use of the limited time which each soldier passes with the colours.

I am convinced that the adoption of my method will as quickly make perfect the education of the men as of the horses.

CHAPTER II

CONTROL AND DISTRIBUTION OF ENERGY

The horse, like all other organised beings, is endowed with a weight and energy which belong exclusively to him. The weight inherent in the body of the animal makes it inactive, and tends to fix it to the ground. The energy, on the contrary, owing to the power which it has of mobilising this weight, of dividing it, and of transferring it from one part of the body to another, imparts movement to the whole being, and regulates its balance, speed and direction.

To make this truth clear, we will take a horse standing still. His body will be in perfect balance, if each of his legs supports exactly the amount of weight which rightly belongs to it in this position. If he wishes to move forward at the walk, he must first transfer to the legs which remain fixed to the ground the weight supported by the leg which he first raises. It is just the same in the other paces: in the trot the translation of weight is from one diagonal to the other; in the gallop from the forehand to the hind quarters, and vice versa. One must, therefore, never confound weight with energy: the latter is determinant, the former subordinate to it. It is by transferring the weight on to certain legs that the energy fixes them to the ground, and mobilises the other legs. The speed at which these translations of weight are made determines the different paces, which are themselves true or false, equal or unequal, according as the transference of weight is carried out evenly or irregularly.

It will be understood that this motive power is subdivided *ad infinitum,* since it is spread over all the muscles of the animal, and when he makes use of it himself the energy is spontaneous, whereas when it is controlled by the rider it is aroused and directed by him. In the first case the rider dominated by his horse is at the mercy of the latter's humour: in the second case, on the contrary, he makes him a docile instrument, and brings him under the supreme control of his will. The horse from the moment he is mounted should therefore place his energy entirely at the disposal of his rider, and the maintenance of this subservience constitutes the greatest talent of the horseman.

But a result such as this cannot be attained at once. The young horse accustomed when at liberty to regulate the employment of his energy himself, will at first submit with difficulty to the outside influence which comes to take full possession of it. A conflict naturally arises between the horse and the rider; and the latter will be conquered if he does not possess the energy, the patience, and especially the necessary knowledge to attain success. The energy of the horse being the element upon which the horseman must principally act to get first control and then direction, it is upon this that he must fix his attention. He will examine what it is and from whence it comes, the parts in which it contracts itself the most with a view to resistance, and the physical causes which bring about this contraction. As soon as he is satisfied on these points, in dealing with his pupil he will only employ means which are in accord with the latter's nature, and his progress will then be rapid.

Unfortunately, search can be made in vain amongst authors, both ancient and modern, who have written about equitation, I will not say for sound principles, but for ideas concerning the energy of the horse. All have written of resistances, of oppositions, of lightness and of balance, but not one of them has thought of telling us what are the causes of resistance, and how we should attack and destroy them, so as to obtain that lightness and balance which they so insistently recommend. It is this omission which has thrown on the principles of equitation so many doubts and so much obscurity; it is this which rendered the art stationary for so long a time, and it is this omission which I now aim at making good.

In the first place I lay it down as a principle that all the resistances of young horses arise in the first place from a physical cause, and that this cause only becomes moral through the want of skill, or the ignorance or brutality of the rider. In fact, outside the natural stiffness common to all these animals, each one of them has a distinctive conformation, which, according to its degree of perfection, constitutes the amount of harmony that exists between the energy and the weight. The want of this harmony occasions the ungainliness of the paces, the difficulty in the movements, in fact, all the obstacles to a good education. In a state of freedom, no matter how badly the horse may be shaped, instinct alone is sufficient to use the energy in a way to maintain the balance; but there are movements impossible to make until a preparatory work has overcome defects of conformation by a better management of the motive power. A horse does not start a movement without first taking a certain position, and if the horse uses his energy to oppose the taking of this position, this resistance must first be overcome and the energy properly directed.

I must impress on amateurs desirous of following my advice to avoid mixing up with it methods which are contrary to it. Amongst these grotesque inventions we find the dumb-jockey, to which some writers have attributed properties which sound horsemanship condemns; in fact, the permanent pressure of the bridoon on the bars of the mouth is a discomfort and not a means of control, and it teaches the horse to get behind the bit in order to avoid its action. Thanks to this brutal force the horse will at an early age learn how to avoid the effects of the rider's hand. It is on the horse's back, and by true and progressive oppositions of hand and legs, that prompt and infallible results will be obtained. It requires intelligence to speak intelligently to a horse, and not a machine acting without motive power.

Now I ask the rider if, before overcoming these first difficulties, he adds the weight of his own body, and his own ill-considered demands, will not the horse experience a still greater difficulty in performing certain movements? Will not the efforts to force the horse to do what is contrary to his nature break themselves against this unsurmountable obstacle? He will naturally resist, and with all the greater success because the bad distribution of his energy will suffice in itself to paralyse the efforts of the rider. The resistance, therefore, arises from a physical cause, and this cause becomes moral the moment the horse commences to contrive for himself means for freeing himself from the restraint imposed on him, by the rider wishing thus to force into action parts of the body which have not been previously suppled by exercises. When things are in this state they cannot but get worse.

The rider, soon disgusted with the powerlessness of his efforts, will blame the horse for his own ignorance, and he will call an animal a brute which, probably possesses brilliant resources, and of which, with more discernment and aptitude, he might have made a riding horse both docile in character, and graceful and comfortable in his paces. I have often remarked that the horses reputed untameable are those which develop the greatest energy and vigour, as soon as the rider has put right the physical defects which impeded their movements. In the case of those which, notwithstanding their bad conformation, have been finally brought by a similar method of training to a semblance of obedience, it is necessary to attribute the success to their natural lack of energy in resistance; if they willingly submit to certain very simple exercises, it is because the rider does not push them too far, knowing that they would quickly find the energy to resist any more exacting demands. The rider will be able to make them move in the different paces; but how irregular, stiff and ungraceful those movements are, and what ridicule do such horses bring upon the poor wretches whom they knock and drag about at their own free will, instead of allowing themselves to be directed by them ! This state of things is quite natural, because one has not destroyed the first cause of its existence, the bad distribution of energy, and the stiffness caused by the bad conformation.

But, some opponent will say, "Since you recognise that the difficulties arise from the conformation of the horse, how is it possible to overcome them? You do not presume to change the structure of the animal, and to reform nature's work? "No, certainly not, but whilst agreeing that it is impossible to increase the width of a narrow chest, to lengthen a neck which is too short, to lower a high croup,

24

to shorten and strengthen loins which are long, feeble and narrow, I none the less maintain that if I destroy the different contractions occasioned by these physical defects, if I supple the muscles, if I make myself master of the horse's energy so as to be able to dispose of it as I wish, it will be easy for me to anticipate any resistance, to give more power and elasticity to feeble parts, to restrain those which are too vigorous, and thus to make amends for the bad effects of an imperfect conformation and character.

I have no fear in saying that similar results were and are impossible with the old methods. But if the science of those who adhere to the old methods fails, when applied to the great number of defective horses, one finds unfortunately certain horses which, owing to their perfect conformation and the resulting ease in education help considerably in perpetuating the useless rule of thumb methods so harmful to the progress of equitation. A well-made horse is one whose parts, harmonising regularly, produce a perfect balance. It is as difficult for a horse thus made to leave his naturally balanced position, to take a badly balanced one and to resist his rider, as it is at first painful to the badly made horse to equally distribute his energy and weight, without which regularity of movement is impossible.

It is, therefore, only in the education of these badly made horses that the real difficulties of horsemanship arise. In the case of well-made horses the training should be, so to speak, instantaneous, as all the means of movement being in their proper place, nothing remains but to stimulate them. This result is obtained by my method much more quickly than under the old method.

If we once admit the following truths:—

That the education of the horse consists in the complete control of his energy ;

That one cannot dispose of this energy except by overcoming all the resistances ;

That the resistances have their origin in the contraction caused by defective conformation; nothing remains to be done but to look for the parts where these contractions occur, in order to try to overcome them and make them disappear.

Long and careful observations have made it clear to me that, whatever the defective conformation which, in the horse, prevents the proper distribution of energy, it is always in the neck that one first feels the effect. There is no wrong movement, no resistance, which is not preceded by the contraction of the muscles of the neck; and as the mouth is so intimately connected with the neck, the stiffness of the one communicates itself instantaneously to the other. These two points are those on which the horse relies for defeating all the efforts of the rider. One can easily understand the great obstacle which they must offer to the control of the rider, since the neck and the head being the two principal levers by which he influences and directs the animal, it is impossible to get him to do anything so long as the rider is not absolute master of these most important and indispensable means of action.

In the hindquarters, the parts in which the energy contracts itself the most for resistance to the rider, are the loins and the croup.

The contractions of the opposite ends of the horse are mutually, the one for the other, cause and effect; that is to say, that the stiffness of the neck brings about that of the quarters, and vice versa. Therefore, oppose the one by the other, and as soon as you have succeeded in overcoming the contractions, and in restoring the balance and the harmony that they prevented between the forehand and the hindquarters, the education of the horse will be half finished. I am now going to explain how one can infallibly succeed in doing this.

CHAPTER III

THE SUPPLING EXERCISES

My principal aim here is to deal with the education of the horse; but this education is so intimately connected with that of the rider that it is impossible to improve the one without the other. In explaining the system which should make a horse perfect, I will of necessity teach the horseman to apply it himself, and it will only remain for him to teach to-morrow that which I have explained to him to-day. There is nevertheless one thing that no teaching can give, and that is that fineness of tact, that delicacy of feeling with the horse, which belong only to privileged organisations, and without which one will seek in vain to pass certain limits. Now let us get back to our subject.

We now know the parts of the horse which contract the most when he wishes to resist his rider, and we understand the necessity of suppling them. Shall we commence by attacking and exercising them all together, in order to master them all at once? No, certainly not, as that would be relapsing into the old methods, and' we are convinced of their inefficacy. The horse is endowed with a muscular power far superior to ours, and we would certainly be defeated if we overexcited the energy in all his different parts at once. Since the contractions have their seat in different parts separated from one another, we must learn how to profit from this division to attack them one at a time, in the same way as a skilled general destroys in detail forces which he could not resist if they were united.

No matter what the age, the disposition and the conformation of my pupil may be, my procedure at first will always be the same. The results, however, will be more or less prompt and easily obtained, according to the perfection of his nature and the influence the hand has, owing to his having previously learnt to obey it. The suppling exercises which in the case of a well formed horse will not have any other aim than to dispose him to submit his energy to our directions, ought also to re-establish calm and confidence when dealing with a badly broken horse, and destroy in a defective conformation the contractions, which arc the cause of resistance and of opposition to a perfect balance. The difficulties to be overcome will be the outcome of these defects, which will all quickly disappear if on our part we exercise a little perseverance. In the progression which we are going to follow in suppling the different parts of the horse, we will naturally commence with the most important, that is to say, the lower jaw and the neck.

The head and the neck of the horse are at the same time the rider's helm and compass. By them he guides the horse, and through them he also feels whether the movement is regular and right. The balance of the whole body is perfect, and the lightness in hand complete when the neck and head themselves are supple and in an easy graceful position. On the other hand, as soon as these parts are contracted there is neither collection nor graceful action. They precede the horse's body in all its forward movements, they make the first preparations, and direct by their attitudes the position that must be taken, and the movement that should be carried out; the rider has not any control over his horse so long as they remain contracted and rebellious; but when once they are supple and under the control of the hand, he is master. If the head and neck arc not the first to begin the changes of direction, if in circular movements they do not bend to the curved line in order to put more or less weight on the right legs to favour the movement, if when going backwards they do not draw themselves in, and if their elevation is not always suitable for the pace the rider desires, the horse will be free to execute or not, as he likes, these movements, because he will remain master of his own energy.

As soon as I had recognised the powerful influence that the stiffness of the neck exercises over the whole mechanism of the horse, I concentrated my mind on finding a remedy. The resistances to the hand are always lateral, upwards or downwards, and I at first-attributed these resistances to the neck alone, endeavouring to supple the horse by frequent flexions in every direction. The result was most gratifying; but although after a time the suppleness of the neck made me absolute master of the energy of the forehand, I still felt a slight resistance which I could not at first understand, and which I finally traced to the lower jaw, and found that the flexibility which I had given to the neck assisted to some extent the contraction of the muscles of this part, by enabling the horse to avoid at times the action of the bit. I set myself therefore at once to find the means of overcoming these resistances of the mouth, and ever since I have always commenced by suppling the lower jaw.

First exercises on foot—the way to make a horse come up to the man and make him quiet to mount.— Before commencing to teach the horse to yield the lower jaw and bend the neck, it is necessary first to give him a lesson in obedience, and to make him appreciate the power of man. This first lesson will quickly make him calm and confident, and will check all the movements which might distract his attention and retard the early education.

Two lessons of half an hour's duration will suffice to secure the preparatory obedience of any horse. The pleasure which this exercise gives to the rider will naturally stimulate him into giving it every day for a few minutes, as it will be as useful to himself as it is instructive to the horse.

The rider should approach his horse with his whip under his arm, quietly and confidently; should speak to him in a low voice, and stroke his face and neck with his hand, and then with the left hand he should take hold of the bit reins, six or seven, inches from the cheeks of the bit, and close his fingers firmly on them so as to strongly oppose the resistance of the horse. The whip should be held in the right hand with the point down, and the rider should gradually raise it to the level of the horse's chest and strike it several times. The first natural movement of the horse will be backwards, and the rider should follow it without reducing the tension on the reins or ceasing to strike the chest with the whip. The rider must maintain absolute self-control, and abstain from showing either in his movements or his face any indication of anger or weakness. Tired out by the effect of this constraint the horse will soon try by another movement to avoid the pain, and it will be by moving forward that he will succeed. The rider should take advantage of this second movement to stop the horse and pat him. The repetition of this exercise will give great results even in the first lesson. The horse having well understood the means by which he avoided the pain, will not await the touch of the whip, and he will soon advance at its slightest movement. The rider should make use of this forward movement to cause the horse to drop his neck and yield his lower jaw, by giving a downward feeling on the bit reins and thus prepare the horse for exercises which follow. The lowering of the neck which I recommend, especially in the case of horses whose withers are considerably higher than the quarters, or who have narrow quarters or feeble loins, is not a position which they should permanently maintain, but it is a means which will help in establishing the balance, which will assist the weak parts, and give them, in consequence, an energy and level movement which they would never have had but for the low position of the neck. As soon as this change of the position of the centre of gravity has been obtained, the horse will become lighter in hand, and then the neck will gradually take an elevated graceful position, without interfering with the easy regular displacement of the weight and transfer of energy. This work is a pleasant recreation, and will moreover help to make the horse stand quietly when being mounted: it will considerably shorten his education and bring on the development of his intelligence. In cases where, owing to his irritable or timid disposition, the horse starts disorderly movements, make use of the cavesson as a means of repression, and administer a few slight jerks. When the horse moves freely forward under the influence of the whip, the time will have come to make a light opposition with the hand holding the bit reins, so as to bring the face of the horse perpendicular with the ground without stopping the forward movement. In this work on foot the whip takes the place of the legs or spurs.

It will be observed that from the commencement of the education, tact is necessary in order to regulate the energy which forces the horse forward, and that which makes him move backward, so as to obtain a commencement of lightness and balance; but to properly carry out this exercise, so apparently simple, thought, calmness and kindness are essential.

The suppling of the lower jaw.—The flexions of the lower jaw, together with the two flexions of the neck which follow, arc taught by the trainer on foot with the horse standing still. The horse should be brought in saddled and bridled, with the reins lying on the neck. The trainer should first sec that the bit is properly placed in the mouth, and that he can pass a finger between the curb chain and the chin. Then, with a kindly expression in his eyes, he should place himself by the horse's head, with his body straight and firm and his feet apart, so as to give him a firm base and enable him to overcome any resistance.

1. To carry out the flexion to the right, the trainer should take hold of the right rein of the bit with the right hand, under the neck six or seven inches from the cheek of the bit, and the left rein with the left hand four inches from the check of the bit. He should then bring his right hand towards his body, whilst extending his left arm so as to turn the bit in the mouth. The force employed should be proportioned to the resistance of the neck and lower jaw alone, so as not to affect the balance which keeps the horse from moving. If the horse moves backwards to avoid the flexion, one should maintain the action of the hands, which

in this case will be carried forward so as to resist the horse's effort and draw him forward. If one has carefully given the lesson with the whip, described above, it will be easy to stop this backward movement, which is a great hindrance to every kind of flexion either of the lower jaw or of the neck.

2. As soon as the flexion has been obtained the left hand should let the left rein slip to the same length as the right, and then the two reins equally stretched will bring the head towards the chest, and hold it there in a perpendicular position until it sustains itself. The horse by tasting the bit will mark his lightness in hand and perfect submission, and the trainer as a recompense should remove the tension of the reins, and allow the horse, after a few seconds, to take his natural position.

The flexion of the jaw to the left should be carried out in the same way, by the trainer standing on the off side of the horse, and he should repeat the flexions first to one side and then to the other.

One will easily understand the importance of these flexions. They train the horse to yield immediately to the slightest pressure of the bit, and to relax the muscles which join the head to the neck. As the head must precede and determine the different positions of the neck, it is indispensable that this latter part should always be subject to the former and accompany its movements. This would only be imperfectly the case if the neck alone were supple, since it would then be the neck which would influence the head and make it follow its movements. That is why at first I experienced, notwithstanding the suppleness of the neck, resistances of which I could not trace the cause. The suppling of the lower jaw, by its action on the bars of the mouth and the head, brings about also the flexion of the neck, and assists considerably in making the horse quickly light in hand.

PLATE I

PLATE II

This exercise is the first attempt which we make to teach the horse to place his energy at our disposal. It is, therefore, very necessary to carry it out with the greatest care so as not to dishearten the horse. If we begin the flexions roughly we shall give the horse a painful experience, as he will not have had the time to understand what is wanted. The opposition of the hands should be gentle, but they should not yield until perfect obedience has been attained, so long as the horse docs not draw himself back; but it will diminish or increase its effect in proportion to the resistance, in such a way as to dominate it without being too exacting. The horse who at first will only yield with difficulty, will finally consider his rider's hand as irresistible, and he will become so used to obeying it, that a simple pressure of the fingers on the reins will suffice to obtain that which at first required all the power of the arms. Each repetition of the lateral flexions will increase the horse's obedience, and when these early resistances diminish in force, the trainer should pass on to the perpendicular flexions, or the lowering of the neck.

The lowering of the neck and direct flexion of the lower jaw.—1. The trainer should place himself by the side of the horse's head; he should take hold of the reins of the bridoon with the left hand six or seven inches from the rings, and the reins of the bit close to the cheeks with the right hand, and he should gently draw the neck down, with the left hand whilst the right hand invites the mobilisation of the lower jaw. He should attentively observe the direction in which he feels resistance; if the horse refuses to lower his head, he should increase the action of his left hand until the horse yields. It should be just the same in all the flexions; the trainer must follow the resistances of the horse in all their changes: for example, if he wishes to bend his horse's head to the right, and the head moves upwards instead of to the side, he should devote all his attention to lowering the head in order to overcome the resistance which alone prevents the lateral movement: this means, judiciously employed, gives infallible and prompt results. (Plate I.)

2. When the horse's head descends of itself and by its own weight, the trainer should immediately cease to use any force, and allow his horse to take his natural position. (Plate II.) This exercise often, repeated will soon supple the muscles which raise the neck, and which play a great part in the resistances of the horse, and will moreover make easy the direct flexions and the mobilisation of the lower jaw, which will follow the lateral flexions. The trainer can carry out this exercise alone; nevertheless, it is a good plan to place an assistant in the saddle so as to accustom the horse to the suppling exercises when mounted. This assistant will merely hold, without stretching them, the bridoon reins in the right hand with the nails down.

The flexions of the lower jaw have already suppled the upper part of the neck, but we have obtained this by means of a powerful and direct motive power, and it is necessary to get the horse to yield to a less direct indication. It is, moreover, important that the suppleness and flexibility, which are principally necessary in the upper part of the neck, should extend to the whole neck so as to completely destroy any stiffness. The downward pull on the bridoon reins only acts through the mountings on the top of the head, and it often takes a long time to get the horse to lower it. In this case the trainer can cross the two bridoon reins by taking the left rein in the right hand, and the right rein in the left hand, at six or seven inches from the horse's mouth, so as to cause a sufficiently strong pressure on the chin. This pressure should continue until the horse yields. (Plate III.) Again, you can act directly on the lower jaw in a way which will make it quickly mobile. Take, say, the left rein of the bit at six or seven inches from the mouth, and draw it directly towards the left shoulder, whilst at the same time drawing the left bridoon rein forward with the left hand in a line level with the right hand. If the horse tries to raise the head, the left hand holding the bridoon rein will give it a downwards tension, and cease this action the instant the horse yields. The two hands thus acting in opposite directions will soon cause the horse to yield his lower jaw. The force employed should always be in proportion to the strength of the resistance. By means of this direct action it will only take a few lessons to produce a suppleness which could not have been obtained so promptly by any other means. (Plate IV.)

Lateral flexions of the neck.—1. The trainer should place himself near the horse's shoulder as when teaching the flexions of the lower jaw; he should take the right bridoon rein, which passes across the horse's neck, with his right hand, so as to establish an intermediate point between the impulsion which he will communicate and the resistance that the horse will show; he should hold the left rein with the left hand about twelve inches from the ring. As soon as the horse tries to avoid the constant tension of the right rein by turning his head to the right, the trainer should let the left rein slip through his hand so as not to restrict the bending of the neck. This left rein should act by a succession of light intermittent touches, every time the horse tries to escape from the action of the right rein by moving his quarters.

2. When the head and the neck have completely yielded to the right, the trainer should give an equal tension to both reins so as to place the head in a perpendicular position. Suppleness and lightness in hand will soon follow this position, and. as soon as the horse has shown the absence of all contraction by tasting the bit. the. trainer should remove the tension of the reins, whilst being careful that the head does not displace' itself roughly on feeling itself free. Should it do so one has merely to check it lightly with the right rein. After keeping the horse for a few seconds in this position, put him back into his original position by feeling the left rein lightly. The important point is that the horse in any of his movements should not take the initiative.

The flexion of the neck to the left will be carried out on the same principles, but by the opposite means. The trainer can repeat with the bit reins that which he has at first done with the bridoon reins: nevertheless the bridoon should always be used at first, as its effect is milder and more direct. If the flexions have been properly carried out on foot, and if they leave nothing to be desired, the flexions will be easily obtained by the rider when mounted. These first exercises are of great importance, and the time spent over them will considerably shorten the duration of the lessons which should follow.

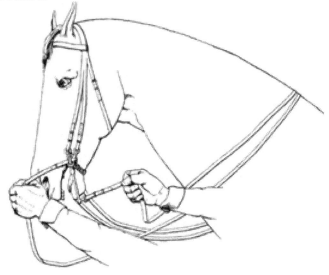

PLATE IV

When the horse submits without resistance to the preceding exercises, it will prove that the suppling of the neck has considerably advanced. The trainer can then continue his work with a less direct means of action, and without the sight of him influencing the horse. He should place himself in the saddle, and commence by renewing with lengthened reins the lateral flexions, with which he has already exercised the horse.

Lateral flexions of the neck, the trainer being in the saddle.—1. To carry out the flexion to the right, the rider should take a bridoon rein in each hand, the left hand only just feeling the mouth, whilst the right hand should have slight feeling at first, and gradually increase the pressure in proportion to the horse's resistance, so as to always dominate him. The horse, tired out by a fight which only produces increased pain, will learn that the only means of avoiding it is to turn his head to the side on which he feels the pressure.

2. As soon as the horse's head has been bent to the right, the left rein will prevent the nose from passing the perpendicular line. One should attach a great importance to the head remaining always in this position. Without this the flexion will be imperfect and the suppleness incomplete. The movement having been properly carried out, a light tension of the left rein will place the horse in his natural position. The flexion to the left will be carried out in the same way, the rider using alternately the bridoon and bit reins.

I have said that the greatest attention should be paid to suppling the upper part of the neck. When once on the horse, and when the lateral flexions are obtained without resistance, the rider should often content himself with a half flexion, the head and the upper part of the neck pivoting on the lower part. This exercise should be frequently repeated, even after the education of the horse is finished, so as to maintain the suppleness and to help getting the horse in hand.

It now remains—to complete the suppling of the head and neck—to overcome the contractions which cause the direct resistances, and prevent the proper placing of the head and neck.

The direct flexions of the head and neck (Ramener).— The rider should at first make use of the bridoon reins, and hold them in the left hand, whilst he places his right hand flat on the reins in front of the left hand, so as to strengthen its action; he should then progressively increase the feeling on the mouth. As soon as the horse yields, the rider has merely to raise his right hand to diminish the tension on the reins and to recompense the horse. The hand should never exert a force greater than the resistance of the neck alone, and one has only to close in the legs lightly so as to fix the hindquarters. When the horse obeys the indications of the bridoon he will yield much more promptly to the action of the bit, the effect of which is more powerful and should consequently be employed with more gentleness than the bridoon. (Plate V.)

2. The horse will have completely yielded to the action of the hand, when his head has been brought into a position perpendicular to the ground; the contraction will then cease, and the horse will make this evident by the mobility of his lower jaw, and by preserving a perfect lightness in hand. The rider, nevertheless, should take care to complete the flexion, and not allow himself to be deceived by the pretences of

the horse, who will at times yield to a quarter or a third of the distance, and then open his mouth and resist. II, for example, the horse's nose, which should follow a curved line of *ten* degrees to reach a perpendicular position, stops at the fourth or sixth degree, and offers further resistance, the hand should follow the movement and then resist firmly, because a concession on its part would encourage resistances and increase the difficulties. It is only when the nose has descended to the tenth degree that the flexion is complete and the balance perfect. The rider should then relax the tension on the reins, but in such a way as to retain the head in this position should it attempt to leave it. If at first he allows the head to re-take its natural position, this should only be in order that the flexion, may be repeated, and to make the horse understand that the perpendicular position is the only one the rider's hand allows him to maintain. At the very start accustom the horse to the pressure of the legs, in order to stop all the backward movements of the body, movements which will put it in his power to avoid the effects of the hand, or to take a position which will increase his power of resistance. (Plate VI.)

This flexion is the most important of all; the others merely prepare the horse for it, and as soon as the horse makes it with ease and promptness, and as soon as a light feeling on the reins is sufficient to bring in the nose and maintain the head in a perpendicular position, we have a proof that the suppling is completed, the contraction destroyed, and lightness and balance established in the forehand. The guidance of this part of the horse from now on will be easy and natural, because we shall have enabled him to understand our indications and to submit to them immediately and without effort. As to the duty of the legs, they should support the hindquarters in order to enable the horse to keep his hind legs well under the body, and so help him to bring his head in, whilst at the same time preventing him from avoiding the effects of the hand by moving backwards. It is necessary to get the horse completely in hand in order to bring the hind legs well under the centre of the body, and so balance the horse perfectly on his forehand and hindquarters, (Rassembler.)

Collection of the horse.—I have published four editions of my method, without devoting a special article to the effects of collecting a horse. Although I myself frequently collect my horse, I had not till lately become aware of the importance of making collection a special part of my instruction. I had not, in fact, attached due importance to this frequent effect of the aids until new experiences forced it upon me.

Collection is the result of a continuous and well-regulated opposition between the hands and the legs. It should aim at bringing into a position of balance all the parts of the horse, and place his direction absolutely in the hand of the rider, who can at once stop any movement in any direction. It is, moreover, by this means that success will be attained in distributing equally the weight of the body over the four legs, and that one will produce momentary immobility. The collection of the horse between the hand and legs should proceed and follow each exercise, and it is essential when employing the aids for this purpose, that the action of the legs should always precede that of the hands, so as to prevent the horse from sinking back on to his hocks, and so fixing himself in a position of resistance. Any movement of his legs, initiated by the horse, under any circumstances whatever, should be stopped by collecting him between the hand and the legs; and whenever the horse becomes unruly, the rider will find in this effect of collection a powerful and infallible correction, and a means of bringing the horse's energy again under his control.

It is by placing all the parts of the horse in the most exact order that the rider will easily communicate the impulsion which will produce the regular movement of the legs: it is then also that he will be able to appeal to the horse's understanding and make him appreciate what is wanted of him; the rider will then secure a moral effect by patting the horse and speaking kindly to him.

Overbending.—Although there are few horses naturally inclined to overbend, one should, nevertheless, when the fault does occur, exercise the horse in all the flexions, even those which lower the neck. In the position called overbent, the horse's chin is brought near to the chest, and remains touching the lower part of the neck; an excessively high croup combined with the permanent contraction of the lowering muscles of the neck is generally the cause. Therefore supple these muscles in order to deprive them of their excessive power, and give to the raising muscles, their antagonists, the predominance which helps and brings the neck into a good and useful position. This being accomplished, teach the horse to move freely forward to the pressure of the legs, and to answer kindly and steadily to their attacks, which will bring the hind legs under the body and lower the croup. One should then endeavour, with the bridoon reins at first and the bit reins after-wards, to raise the horse's head; to do this, hold the hand somewhat high, and at some distance from the body, and maintain an upward pressure on the mouth until the horse yields by raising his neck. As this kind of horse has generally little action, the rider must be very careful that his hand has not any backward effect, and so take from the impulsion necessary for the movement. The pace, commencing with the walk, must preserve its energy whilst the hand endeavours to raise the neck. This precept is applicable in all the changes which the hand causes the neck to make 5 and it is especially essential when dealing with a horse; inclined to overhead. Further, remember that the horse has two ways of replying to the pressure of the bit;

he can yield and relieve himself of the pressure by recoiling into himself: this kind of surrender can but prejudice his education, because if the hand strengthens itself too much, if it does not wait until the horse changes of himself the position of his head, the backward movement of the body will precede and be accompanied by a transfer of weight to the hindquarters. In this case the contraction of the neck will not be removed The proper cessioa which helps so much the rapid and positive education of the horse, is obtained by giving a half or three-quarters tension to the reins,, and then closing the fingers very strongly on them, without bringing the hand nearer to the body. Soon, the pressure of the hand helped by a constant pressure of the legs, will cause the horse to answer to this light and steady pressure of the bit by yielding his head and neck *only,* and the action of the rider will only have effect on the energy necessary to carry out the displacement. It is by this means that he will place the body of the horse straight, and through it will obtain that balance which until now has not been attained in its most perfect form.

To sum up what we have just explained about a horse which overbends, we will repeat that it is by producing an energetic forward movement with the legs, combined with an *upward* action of the hand, that one will succeed in a short time in improving the carriage and movements of the horse. Finally, whatever may have been the original position of the neck, it is by first obtaining the ready lowering of the neck that one quickly attains its perfect elevation.

The bit and sensibility of the mouth.—I will finish this chapter by a few reflections upon the supposed difference of sensibility of the horse's mouth, and the kind of bit which best suits it.

I still ask myself how one has been so long able to attribute merely to the difference in conformation of the bars, the lightness or heaviness in hand which is found in horses. How has one been able to think that according to the thickness of the flesh between the bit and the bone; of the lower jaw the horse either yields to the slightest indication of the hand, or runs away, notwithstanding the most vigorous efforts of a strong pair of arms? It is, nevertheless, by relying on this inconceivable error that there have been forged bits of the most ridiculous and varied shapes, real instruments of torture, the effect of which could not but increase the trouble which it was sought to remedy.

If any one had taken the trouble to examine the cause of the resistances, he would soon have recognised that this, like all the others, does not arise from the difference in conformation of a feeble organ like the bars, but from the contraction communicated to the different parts of the horse, and especially to the neck, by some grave defect in conformation. It is, therefore, futile to hang on to the reins, and to place in the horse's mouth an instrument more or

50

less cruel; the mouth will remain insensible to our efforts, so long as Ave have not given it the suppleness which alone will enable it to yield.

I therefore lay it down as a principle, that there does not exist any difference of sensibility in the mouths of horses, that all have the same sensitiveness when the head is properly placed, and offer the same resistance in proportion as the line of the face leaves the vertical position.

There are horses which are heavy in hand; but this heaviness arises from the length or weakness of the loins, from a narrow croup, short quarters, small thighs, and straight hocks, or finally, from the croup being much higher or lower than the withers; these are the real causes of resistance; the contraction of the neck, the fixity of the jaws are merely the effects; the bars have nothing to do with the difficulties. By suppling the neck and the lower jaw, this hardness disappears completely. Experiences, a hundred times repeated, give me the right to boldly advance this principle, which perhaps at first will seem too absolute, but which is none the less true.

I consequently only recognise one kind of bit, and I here give the shape and dimensions which I recommend as making it as simple as it is mild.

The cheeks should be 6 ¼ inches long from the eye to the end of the cheeks: the circumference of the canons 2 ¼ inches: the liberty for the tongue If inches at the bottom and

¾ inch at the top, and the width of the bit should alone vary, according to the width of the horse's mouth..

I affirm that this bit will secure the most absolute obedience from any horse that has been properly prepared by suppling exercises, and I need not add, since I deny the utility of severe bits, that I reject all means outside the resources of the rider himself, such as martingales, etc.

CHAPTER IV

SUPPLING THE HINDQUARTERS

The rider in directing his horse acts directly on two of his parts: the forehand and hindquarters, and in doing so he employs two agents—the legs which give impulsion to the croup, the hands which direct and regulate this impulsion by means of the head and neck. A perfect accord should therefore always exist between these two powerful agencies, but a similar harmony is equally necessary between the parts of the horse, which they are each especially intended to influence. However much one tries to make the head and neck flexible and light, and obedient to the indications of the hand, the results will be incomplete and the balance imperfect, so long as the hindquarters remain heavy, contracted and rebellious to the direct agent which ought to control them.

I have explained by what simple and easy means one can give to the forehand the qualities which are indispensable to proper directive control; it now remains for me to explain how one can educate the hindquarters in a similar way, so as to complete the suppling of the horse, and restore balance and harmony by the development of all his means of movement. The resistances of the neck and those of the croup mutually assisting one another, our work will be all the more easy owing to our already having overcome the former.

Flexions and mobilisation of the croup.—(1) The rider should hold the bit reins in the left hand, and those of the bridoon crossed the one over the other in the right hand with the nails turned down; he should first bring back the horse's head into the perpendicular position by a light action of the bit; then, if he wishes to carry out the movement to the right, he should carry the left leg back behind the girths, and place it against the horse's flank, and fix it there till the croup yields to its pressure. The rider should use at the same time the bridoon rein, on the same side as the leg, and proportion its effect to the resistance opposed. Of these two forces, exerted by the left rein and the leg of the same side, the first is intended to overcome the resistances, and the second to determine the movement. At first one will be content with only one or two steps to the side. (Plate VII.)

(2) The croup having acquired greater ease in mobilising itself, one will be able to continue the movement in such a way as to complete pirouettes on the forehand to the right or left. As soon as the quarters yield to the pressure of the leg, the rider in order to attain the perfect balance of the horse, should now make use of the rein on the opposite side to this leg. Its effect, at first light, will be progressively increased until the head is inclined to the side to which the croup is moving. (Plate VIII.)

To thoroughly explain this movement, I will add some explanations, all the more important because they are applicable to all equitation exercises.

The horse, in all his movements, cannot maintain a perfect and constant balance without a combination of opposed forces skilfully harmonised by the rider. In the turn on the forehand, for example, if, when the horse has yielded to the pressure of the leg, the rider continues the indication of the rein of the same side as this leg, it is evident that he will over-reach his aim, because he will be using a force which is now superfluous. It is therefore necessary to establish two motive agencies, the effects of which balance without opposing one another; a result which is attained in the pirouette by the tension of the rein on the opposite side to the leg. Accordingly commence with the rein and the leg of the same side, say the left, until it is time to pass to the second part of the exercise, then use the bit rein held in the left hand, and lastly the bridoon rein of the side opposite to the leg. The horse's energy is now under diagonal control and consequently the balance is natural and the execution of the movement easy. The horse's head being inclined towards the side to which the croup is moving, adds to the gracefulness of the exercise, and gives the rider greater facility in regulating the activity of the hindquarters, and in maintaining the shoulders in their place. Tact alone will be able to indicate the use he ought to make of his leg and the rein, so that their effects mutually assist instead of opposing one another.

There is not any reason for me to repeat that during the whole of this exercise, as in all others, the neck should remain supple and light, the head in a perpendicular position, and the lower jaw mobile, whilst the hand holding the bit reins keeps them thus; the right hand with the help of the bridoon overcomes the lateral resistances, and determines the various inclinations of the head and neck, until the horse is sufficiently trained to obey the simple pressure of the bit. If, in overcoming the contractions of the quarters, we allowed the horse to transfer the stiffness to the forehand, our efforts would be futile, and the results of our first exercises lost. We will, on the other hand, assist the supplying of the hindquarters by preserving the advantages which we have already acquired over the forehand, and by keeping isolated the contractions which we have still to overcome. The rider's leg on the opposite side to the one which determines the rotation of the croup should also be closed in during the movement, so as to keep the horse in his place by communicating a forward impulsion, which the other leg makes use of to move the horse to the left or right. There will thus be at the same time a force which keeps the horse in position and another which effects the rotation. In order that the pressure of the two legs may not oppose one another, whilst being used at the same time, the rider should place the leg that moves the croup further behind the girths than the other, which will remain closed in with a force equal to that of the active leg. The action of the legs will then be distinct; the one will press the horse towards the left, whilst the other will press him forward, and it is with the assistance of this latter leg that the hand places and fixes the forehand.

Although this exercise is elementary, it will nevertheless train the horse to carry out easily at the walk all the school paces on two lines. After eight days' moderate exercise, one will thus accomplish without effort, a work which the old school did not dare to attempt till two or three years had been given up to teaching and experiments.

When the rider has taught the horse's croup to yield promptly to the pressure of the legs, he will be able to mobilise or immobolise it at will, and will consequently be able to execute the turns on the hindquarters. To teach these he should take a bridoon rein in each hand, the one will serve to incline the neck and shoulders to the side to which the turn is desired, the other to help the leg on the other side, if it is unable to hold the croup in its place. At first this leg should be placed as far back as possible and abstain from using any pressure unless the croup moves to that side. A movement well controlled will bring about prompt results, but at first the rider should be satisfied with a few well-executed steps, and then stop his horse by enclosing him between the hand and the legs; he should then immediately yield to the horse; one here supposes five or six stops during the complete rotation of the shoulders round the croup. If this movement is executed slowly and carefully, and if the horse is light in hand the whole time, I guarantee surprising results. All my pupils, when left to themselves, or those who practise with the aid of a book only, often experience checks or slow progress in the education of their horses, and the cause of this is that they often pass too quickly from one exercise to another. Take time to secure speed, that is the great precept, and, if it is practised with intelligence, it will give infallible results.

Work in a stationary position now terminates, and I am going to explain how one will complete the suppling of the hindquarters, whilst at the same time commencing to combine their action with that of the forehand.

The "rein-back."—This is an exercise the importance of which has not been sufficiently appreciated, but which nevertheless will have a great influence on the education of the horse. If practised according to the old teaching, there would not be any success, since the series of exercises which ought to precede it were not known. The rein-back essentially differs from that bad retrograde impulsion which moves the horse backwards with the croup contracted and the neck stretched out; this is nothing but jibbing. The true backward movement supples the horse and adds grace and precision to his natural paces. The first condition, to obtain it, is that the horse must be in hand, that is to say, supple, light in his forehand, square on his legs, and balanced in every part, and this balance will be shown by a perfect lightness. The horse thus placed will easily be able to give, to his fore and hind legs, mobility and an equal elevation.

The rider will now be able to appreciate the good effects and the indispensable necessity of suppling the neck and quarters. The rein-back, painful at first to the horse, will always incline him to resist the effects of the hands by stiffening the neck, and the effects of the legs by the contraction of the croup; these are instinctive resistances. If we are not able to forestall these bad tendencies, how shall we obtain the backward and forward movement of weight, which alone will bring about the perfect execution of the movement? If the impulsion, which for the backward movement should come from the forehand, exceeds its proper limits, the movement will become painful, impossible, and will cause sudden and violent movements on the part of the horse, and resistances at first physical, afterwards moral, and always disastrous to his organisation.

On the other hand, the displacements of the croup, by destroying the harmony which ought to exist between the reciprocally related forces of the forehand and hindquarters, would also prevent the proper execution of the rein-back. The preparatory exercise, to which we have subjected the horse, will make it easy to keep the croup in a line with the shoulders, in order to maintain the necessary translation of energy and weight from one to the other.

The rider, to commence the movement, should first of all satisfy himself that the quarters arc in line with the shoulders, and that the horse is light in hand; he should then lightly close in his legs, to cause the horse to raise one of his hind legs, and to prevent the body from moving before the neck. It is then that the direct pressure of the bit by forcing the horse to carry his balance back will cause the first backward step. As soon as the horse obeys, the rider should case the hand immediately to reward the horse, and so as not to force the action of the forehand. If the croup leaves the straight line, he should bring it back with the pressure of the leg aided, if necessary, by the bridoon rein of the same side.

Now that I have defined that which I call the true backward movement, I should explain what I mean by "behind the hand." This movement is too painful for the horse, too ungainly, and too much opposed to the proper development of his mechanism for it not to have been noticed by every man interested in horsemanship. We place the horse behind the hand, whenever we carry back too much of the weight on to the hindquarters, and by thus destroying the balance make gracefulness of movement impossible. Lightness in hand is the base of all true movement. It will be understood from this that the difficulty in horsemanship does not consist in the direction to be given to the horse, but in giving him the right position, which will alone remove all difficulties. In effect, if the horse executes a movement, it is the rider who places him for it, and therefore the latter is to blame for all irregular movement. It is sufficient to give a horse live minutes' exercise in the rein-back on eight consecutive days to teach him to execute it with ease. The rider should at first be satisfied with one or two steps to the rear, and then enclose his horse between the hands and legs, gradually increasing the number of steps, until the horse can move backwards as easily as forwards.

What a great stride we shall then have made in the education of our pupil! At first the defective conformation of the horse, his natural contractions, the resistances which we encountered, seemed as if they would for ever defy our efforts. They would doubtless have been in vain, if we had employed bad methods; but the carefully thought-out progression of our training, the destruction of the horse's initiative, the suppling and bringing under control of all rebellious parts, have enabled us to dominate the whole mechanism of the horse, and to produce suppleness, ease, and harmony, between parts which, owing to their bad disposition, seemed fated to continually oppose one another; finally, eight or ten days are sufficient to obtain these important results. Have not I then reason for saying that, if it is not in my power to change the defective conformation of a horse, I can nevertheless prevent the bad effects of these physical defects, to the point of enabling him to execute gracefully and naturally the same movements as the best-made horse? By suppling the parts of a horse on which the rider acts directly in order to dominate and guide him, by training them to yield easily, and without hesitation, to the various indications which may be conveyed to them, I have, in fact, destroyed their stiffness, and brought the centre of gravity to its proper place, the middle of the body. I have, moreover, solved the greatest difficulty in horsemanship, that of subduing the parts on which the rider acts directly, in order to give him infallible means of control over his horse, and it is only by destroying the horse's initiative, and in suppling the various parts of his body, that one will arrive at this result. One thus entrusts to the discretion of the rider all the horse's means of action, but this will not suffice to make him a perfect horseman. The control of energy, which is thus given him, demands for the execution of the different paces, much study and ability, and I will explain in the following chapters the rules to be observed. I will now terminate this chapter by a rapid summing up of the progression to follow in the suppling exercises.

Stationary work, training on foot—The forehand.— (1) Flexions of the lower jaw to the right and left with the bit reins.

(2) Direct flexions of the lower jaw, and lowering of the neck, this lowering exercise should be all the more insisted on if the hindquarters show signs of being weaker than the forehand. It is most necessary to overcome all tendencies and irregular movement. It is by making a horse light in hand that we thus succeed in transforming him; it is results such as these that make horsemanship the most sublime of all the arts.

(3) Lateral flexions of the neck, first with the bridoon reins and then with those of the bit.

Stationary work mounted—The forehand.—(1) Lateral flexions of the neck, first with the bridoon reins, and then with those of the bit.

(2) Direct flexion of the head, first with the bridoon reins, and then with those of the bit.

The hindquarters.—(3) Lateral flexions, and mobilisation of the croup round the shoulders.

(4) Moving the shoulders round the quarters.

(5) Enclosing the horse between the hands and legs.

(6) The rein-back.

I have placed the movement of the shoulders round the quarters amongst stationary exercises, but as it is a movement both complicated and difficult for the horse, one should not carry it out completely until the horse has got his balance in the walk and trot, and can cadence these paces, and until he can carry out changes of direction with ease.

CHAPTER V

THE USE OF THE HORSE'S ENERGY—BY THE RIDER

When the suppling exercises have trained the instinctive energy of the horse up to the point at which he yields it entirely to us, the horse will be a passive machine in our hands, awaiting before doing anything, the impulsion which we may be pleased to communicate to him. It will then be for us, having absolute control of his means of action, to combine them in the proportion necessary for the perfect performance of the movement we wish carried out. The young horse, at first stiff and awkward in the use of his limbs, will require to be carefully trained in order to develop them. In this, as in all other cases, we will follow the rational progression, which commences with the simple before passing on to the complex. We have by the exercises already given, confirmed our means of control: we must now devote our attention to making it easy for the horse to carry out our wishes by exercising all his means of action. If the horse answers to the rider's aids with the lower jaw, the neck, and the quarters; if he yields by placing the whole of his body at the disposition of the impulsion communicated to him; if the movement of his legs is easy and regular, the entire mechanism will have a perfect harmony at the different paces; consequently these are the indispensable qualities to be developed by education. One must not forget that the hand and the legs have also their language, the conciseness of which is admirable. This language, secret and laconic, is comprised in a few words: "You are doing wrong: "This is what you must do"; "You are doing right." It is, therefore, sufficient for the rider to arrive at translating, by means of the aids, the meaning of these three different observations, in order to possess the whole of equestrian knowledge, and to share it with his horse.

The walk.—The walk is the mother of all the paces; it is by it that we obtain the cadence, the regularity, and the extension of the others; but the rider before arriving at these brilliant results, must display as much knowledge as tact. The preceding exercises have trained the horse to answer to the combined effects of hands and legs, which would have been impossible before his instinctive resistances had been destroyed; we have now only to deal with the passive resistances arising out of the horse's weight, and the energy which does not become active until it is put into motion by the rider.

Before starting the walk, one should first assure oneself that the horse is light in hand, that is to say, that his head is perpendicular, his neck supple, his quarters in line with his shoulders, and that he is standing square on his legs. The rider should then gradually close in his legs to produce the necessary impulsion; but he should not yield his hand as taught under the old methods, because the horse, free from all restraint, would lose his lightness, contract himself and render powerless the effect of the hand. The rider should always remember that his hand must be an impassable barrier every time that the head and neck try to leave the balanced position. The horse should never make the attempt without experiencing pain, and it should only be when his head is vertical, or within this line, that he is at ease. The application of my method, therefore, brings the rider to constantly ride his horse with half-stretched reins, except when he wishes to rectify a wrong movement, or to start a new one. When I was staying in Berlin, I saw German, horsemanship practised in all its entirety, and, as I have no wish to pose as a critic, I will merely say that the principles practised in Prussia are diametrically opposed to mine: for instance, several officers who were noted as horsemen said to me, "We like our horses to be in front of the hand," and my reply to them was that I like them to be behind the hand and in front of the legs, so that the centre of gravity is placed between these two aids, as it is only on this condition that the horse is absolutely under the control of the rider, that his movements will be graceful and regular, and that he will change easily from a fast pace to a slow one whilst preserving his balance; because, as I told them, every horse who is in front of the hand is behind the legs, and consequently escapes control at both ends, so his movements cannot be either graceful or regular: furthermore, if he has a vicious conformation, how will you put it right? By proceeding in this way you will never obtain any results. All the theories put into practice before mine consist in giving, with more or less trouble, a direction to the natural energy of the horse without changing the employment of that energy, or improving the bad position of the centre of gravity; means which are indispensable for the creation of a new and perfect balance. These results, however, cannot be obtained otherwise than by the application of my principles: this may be annoying to my opponents, but in these alone lies real horsemanship. The walk, as I have said, should precede the other paces, because the horse having three feet on the ground has less action than in the trot or gallop, and it is consequently easier to regulate and harmonise it. The first suppling exercises should be followed by a few turns round the school at a walk, but only as a relaxation, the rider devoting his attention rather to keeping the head perpendicular with the ground during the walk, than in developing the horse's action. Little by little he increases his demands, and he should secure not only the balance of the horse, but the evenness of action and cadence which alone gives brilliancy in any of the paces. He will commence by light oppositions of the hands and legs, so as to combine the energy of the forehand and hindquarters. This exercise, by teaching the horse to always yield his energy to the direction of his rider, will be as useful in forming his intellect as in developing his limbs and muscles. What pleasures will the skilled horseman find in the progressive study of his art ! His pupil, at first rebellious, will gradually submit himself to his every wish and become like him in character, in fact, his living self; therefore take care: if your horse is capricious, violent or wayward, we shall be right in saying that you are not remarkable yourself for a good disposition, or for skill in handling your horse.

In order that the cadence and speed of the walk may be even and regular, it is indispensable that the impulsive and regulating energy of the rider should also be perfectly harmonised. Suppose, for example, that the rider, in order to press his horse forward at the walk, and to keep him balanced at this pace, employs a force equal to forty pounds, say thirty to produce the impulsion and ten to keep the head in position. If the legs increase their pressure without the hands increasing their action in the same proportion, it is evident that the increased energy communicated would be thrown on to the neck, causing contraction and destroying the balance. If, on the other hand, the hand used too much force, this can only be at the expense of the impulsive force necessary to maintain the pace, which finding itself interfered with, slows down, whilst at the same time the carriage of the horse will lose both grace and energy.

This short explanation will suffice to explain the harmony which ought always to exist between the legs and the hands. It is well understood that their effect should vary according as the construction of the horse obliges him to support more or less of his weight on the forehand or hindquarters; but the rule remains the same though the proportions may be different.

So long as the horse does not remain supple and balanced at the walk, the rider will continue to exercise him on a straight line, but as soon as he has acquired more ease and self-assurance the rider will commence to make him carry out changes of direction to the right and left at the walk.

The changes of direction.—The part played by the hands in the changes of direction is too simple to require explanation here. I will merely remark that the rider should always forestall the resistances of the horse, by distributing his energy so that it maintains the direction of the movement. The rider will, therefore, cause the head and neck to bend with the bridoon rein of the side to which he wishes to turn, and then the bridle will complete the movement. The general rule is that one should always overcome the lateral resistance of the neck with the bridoon, whilst taking care not to commence the turn till the opposition to it has been overcome. If the employment of the hands is much the same now as in the past, it is not the same with the legs; their effect will be totally different from that attributed to them in the old school of horsemanship, and this innovation is so natural that I have difficulty in understanding why it had not been applied before my time. It is by carrying the hand to the right, and by closing in the right leg, they used to tell me, that one turns the horse to the right. With me practice has always preceded thought, and I will now explain how I discovered the fallacy of this principle. However well-balanced my horse might be when working on a straight line, I used to notice that the lightness lost some of its nicety when moving on a contracted circle, although my outside leg assisted the inside one. As soon as the hind leg moved in order to follow the shoulders in the circle, I immediately felt a slight resistance. I then thought of changing the use of my aids, and of closing in the leg on the side opposite to that of the turn. At the same time, instead of at once carrying the hand to the right in order to influence the shoulders, I first established with the hand the necessary opposition to fix the quarters and distribute the energy so as to maintain the balance during the movement. This method was crowned with complete success, and when I consider what part each extremity should play in the changes of direction, I recognise that it is the only sound one.

In fact, when turning to the right, for example, it is the off hind leg which serves as pivot, and supports the whole weight, whilst the near hind leg and the fore legs will describe a circle more or less large. In order that the movement may be correct and free, it is necessary that the pivot on which the body turns should not be inconvenienced: now this is just the result of employing simultaneously the right hand and the right leg. The balance will be compromised and the regularity of the turn made impossible. There is, however, a case in which it is necessary to use the right leg when turning to the right, and that is when, in the turn, the hindquarters remain too much to the right, the right leg then should be closed in with greater strength than the left, otherwise it would form a support which would make painful, perhaps impossible, the rotation of the shoulders round the quarters. The principles, the most exclusive, are subject to some variations.

As soon as the horse carries out easily the changes of direction at the walk, whilst maintaining a perfect balance, the rider can commence to work him at the trot.

The trot.—The rider will commence this pace quietly by following exactly the same method as in teaching the walk. He will keep his horse light in hand, remembering that the faster the pace the more the horse is inclined to fall back into his natural contractions. The hand should therefore exert greater skill in order to always maintain the same lightness, without at the same time interfering with the impulsion necessary for the movement. The legs should assist the hand, and the horse, enclosed between these two barriers, which only interfere with bad tendencies, will soon develop all his best qualities and will acquire with the cadence of the movement, the grace, extension and Sureness, which are inherent in a right balance of the body. Although some people, who have not taken the trouble to thoroughly understand my method, have maintained that it prevents the full extension and the speed of the trot, it none the less remains a fact that a well-balanced horse can trot faster than one which has not this advantage. In fact the indispensable condition of good trotting is the perfect balance of the horse's body, a balance which maintains the regular movement of the diagonal legs, and gives them an equal elevation and extension, together with a lightness, which enables the horse to easily execute all the changes of direction, to slow down and stop, or to increase the pace without effort. The forehand has not then the appearance of towing the hindquarters, which are as far away as possible; every movement becomes easy and graceful, because, the horse's energy being properly distributed, the rider is able to get all the different parts to mutually assist one another. It would be impossible to mention all the horses which have been sent me to train, and whose paces had been so spoiled that it was impossible for them to trot even the shortest distance. A few lessons have always sufficed to make the paces of these horses regular, and I now give you the method I employed.

The difficulty which the horse experiences in keeping himself united in the trot, nearly always arises from the hindquarters. Either this part is feeble, or the superior power in the forehand paralyses it; in either case it is powerless, and causes the movement to be irregular. There is, therefore, either weakness in one extremity or excessive power in the other. The remedy in both cases will be the same, viz. the lowering of the neck, which by decreasing the power of the forehand re-establishes the balance of the two parts. As we have practised this suppling exercise on foot, it will be easy to repeat it on horseback. *Now is seen the utility of this perpendicular flexion which enables one to give an equal power of action to both ends of the horse, so as to harmonise them and bring about regularity in their action.* The horse being thus placed, his fore and hind legs will have time to change from the flexed to the extended position before the weight of the body forces them to come to the ground. If this and other principles developed in this book are properly carried out, one will be able to place amongst the best horses, animals which, owing to their inferiority, were looked upon as screws, and which the old methods would never have raised from their degraded position. It will be sufficient, in order to make a horse into a good trotter, to exercise him in this pace for five minutes each lesson. When he has acquired the ease and lightness necessary, the rider will be able to make him turn round on his hindquarters, and to work on two lines in the walk and trot. I have said that trotting for five minutes will be sufficient at first, because it is less the continuance of an exercise than the accuracy with which it is carried out that produces the perfect execution. The horse will submit more willingly to efforts which are guided and of short duration, and his intelligence also, by becoming familiar with this effective progression, will hasten the final result. He will cheerfully and calmly submit himself to work which does not cause him pain, and one will be able to push his education to the farthest limit, whilst not only preserving his physical organisation, but also restoring organs to their normal state, which under forced work would have deteriorated. This regular development of all the horse's organs will give him not only gracefulness, but also energy and health, and so prolong the period of his usefulness whilst increasing a hundredfold the pleasure of a true horseman.

I do not agree with those who think that the qualities of a horse and the speed of his trot depend principally on the elevation of the withers. I think that in order that a horse may be brilliant and regular in his action the croup and the withers should be on the same level as used to be the case with English horses.[*]

_*_ This is why Baucher so strongly recommends the exercise in lowering the neck for horses that are too high in the withers, or weak *in* the quarters.

CHAPTER VI

CONCENTRATION OF THE HORSE'S ENERGY

Concentrating the horse's energy—by the rider.—
The rider now understands that the only means of obtaining the cadence and the regularity of the walk and trot is to keep the horse perfectly light in hand and balanced. When he is certain of this lightness in hand, when walking on a straight line, when changing direction, and moving in a circle, it will be easy to preserve it when working on two lines.

Attacks of the legs and spurs.—The attacks, so say the authors of books and the professors of equitation, punish a horse when he does not answer to the legs, or when he refuses to approach an object of which he is frightened. According to them the spur is not an aid, but a means of punishing: according to my method, it is a powerful auxiliary, without which it would be impossible to thoroughly train any horse. What! some one will say, you attack with the spur horses which are sensitive, irritable, full of action and fire, horses whose energetic nature disposes them to run away, notwithstanding the strongest bits and the most powerful arms? Yes, and it is with the spurs that I calm the most excitable horses, and that

I bring them up short in their most impetuous rushes. It is with the spur, aided by the hand, that I make graceful the most unpromising natures, and that I succeed in perfecting the education of the most unmanageable horse. The use of the attacks demands, it is true, prudence, tact and gradation, but their effect is invaluable. Now that I have proved the efficacy of my method, now that I see my adversaries, even the most determined, warm partisans of my principles, I have not any fear in developing a method, which I consider *one of the best results* of *my long* study of equitation.

There is not any more difference in the sensibility of the flanks of different horses, than *in* the sensibility of their mouths, that is to say, the direct effect of the spur is generally speaking the same on all I have already shown that the organisation of the bars of the mouth have not anything to do with the resistance to the hand. The supposed hardness of the mouth arises from the bad position *given* to the head by the stiffness of the neck, and by the bad conformation of the loins and quarters of the horse. If we carefully examine the causes which produce that which one calls the sensibility of the flanks, we shall find that it has very nearly the same cause. The greater or less sensitiveness of the horse arises from his animation, from his bad conformation, and from the bad position which is the consequence. When a horse is endowed with a natural animation, with long and feeble loins, and disconnected hindquarters, every backward movement is difficult and the inclination to throw his weight on to his forehand helps him to escape from the pain caused by the spur. He resorts to this movement whenever he feels the rider's leg approaching his sides; and far from being a sensitive horse, he is distracted and desperate. The more he fears the spur, the more he throws himself on to the hand, and defeats the means intended to reduce him to obedience. One has everything to fear from such a horse; he will shy at objects simply because he finds it so easy to avoid them. Now, since his fear arises, one might say, from the bad position the rider allows him to take, it will disappear the moment one remedies the primary cause. It is necessary to control the energy, in order to prevent any displacement of the body, to separate the physical side of the horse from the moral side, and to compel the impressions to concentrate themselves in his brain.

The best proof that the quickness with which a horse replies to the pressure of the legs and spurs is not caused by the sensibility of the flanks, but rather by greater animation combined with bad conformation, is that this same animation is not so marked in a *well-formed* horse, and that the latter endures the attacks much better than a horse whose balance and organisation are of an inferior order. But the spur is, not merely useful in moderating the excessive energy of excitable horses; its effect will equally overcome the inclination which makes a horse throw his centre of gravity too far forward or backward; it is still the spur which I use to make horses sensitive which are lacking in courage and vivacity. In the case of keen horses the energy of the hindquarters is greater than that of the forehand, whereas it is the opposite in the case of spiritless horses, and this accounts for the speed of the former, and the slowness and sluggishness of the latter.

We have, by the suppling exercises, obtained complete possession of the horse's energy, and we must now devote our attention to bringing the centre of gravity to the middle of the horse's body by combining the action of the legs and hands. The superiority which we now possess over the horse will enable us to overcome, at the moment they show themselves, the resistances which tend to make the horse leave the straight position, which is indispensable for the practice of direct suppling exercises. It is also of the first importance that we should put into our work tact and gradation, so that, for example, the legs never communicate an impulsion too great for the hands to take hold of and master at once. I am going to make this principle clearer by a short explanation.

We will take a horse at the walk, employing an energy of 40 lbs., necessary to keep the pace regular. We now apply a gentle gradual pressure of the legs which adds 10 lbs. to the impulsion of the pace. The horse being perfectly light in hand, the hand will immediately feel this increase of energy and it should take hold of it and fix it in the centre of the horse. The legs, meanwhile, will maintain their pressure in order that the energy thus carried back does not return whence it came, simply producing a backward and forward movement of energy. This alternate action of legs and hands will soon collect a great amount of energy in the middle of the horse's body, and will constitute the centre of gravity, and the more one increases it, the more the horse will cease to make an instinctive use of his energy. Soon, when the pressure I of the legs has become insufficient to obtain the collection of the whole energy, the moment will have come to have recourse to a more powerful means, that is to say the attack of the spurs.

One should not attack with the spurs until the horse is well in hand; it will then be easy to intercept the energy aroused by the legs for the benefit of the balance; but it Is necessary to use the spurs with lightness and discretion, they should not be driven In harshly or with much movement of the legs. The rider should close In his legs so that the spurs are quite near the sides without actually touching them. The light touches, with which one commences, should always have the hand for echo; the fingers should therefore be firmly closed on the reins, so as to offer a resistance equal to the energy aroused by the spurs. If the hand fails to intercept the increased impulsion and the general commotion arising from it, the rider before recommencing should re-establish the balance and restore calm to the movements.

By combining the action of the legs and hands, one can progressively increase the force of the attacks until the horse supports them, even when delivered with the greatest vigour, without offering the least resistance to the hand, without Increasing the speed, and without moving the body if one is doing stationary work.

The horse thus trained to the spur is three-quarters trained, since the rider will have the free disposition of all his energy; *moreover, the centre of gravity, in which the energy controlling all parts of the body concentrates itself has been brought to its proper place, the middle of the horse's body.* All the contractions of the horse, useful to movement, are in the rider's control, and he will be able to easily transfer I the weight so as to produce the different paces.

It is now easy to understand the point from which all resistance starts: whether the horse kicks, rears, | or runs away, the wrong position of the centre of gravity is aways the cause. This cause itself arises from a defective construction which one cannot change, it is true, but of which one can always modify the effects. If the horse kicks, the centre of gravity is in the shoulders, when he rears it is in the hindquarters, and when he runs away it is too much in front of the middle of the body. The rider should, therefore, be wholly occupied in always preserving the centre of gravity in the middle of the horse's body, since by so doing, he will prevent resistances, and he will bring the energy of a badly made horse to the spot it occupies in well-made ones. It is this which makes me say that a well-made horse cannot give himself up to resistances or disorderly movements because it will require extraordinary efforts to destroy the harmony of all his means of action, and to give a sufficient displacement of the centre of gravity. Consequently, when I speak of the necessity of giving a horse anew balance to guard against resistances and to remedy his defective formation, I mean to indicate the concentration of energy of which I have been treating, that is, the moving of the centre of gravity from one place to another.

The whole education of the horse lies in this result: when the rider succeeds in obtaining it, his talent becomes perfect, since he changes awkwardness into gracefulness and gives elegance and lightness to movements previously heavy and irregular.

I have often proved that horses said to be cold or pegged shouldered, have not the supposed fault, in other words, that it is extremely rare that they are paralysed in their shoulders in such a way as to interfere with the regularity and speed of their paces, especially so far as the trot is concerned. There exists, without doubt, certain local defects which affect the shoulders, but this is rare; the defect if there is one, arises from the hindquarters. For my part, I have never met with horses said to be paralysed in the shoulders that I have not made free in their movements, and that, after fifteen days' work of half an hour per days' The means are, like all those that I employ, of the greatest simplicity. They consist In suppling the neck so as to get the horse quickly in hand; then with the help of the legs and light touches of the spurs, I bring the hind legs well under the body, the hocks, having then great powers of propulsion, drive the body forward with greater energy, and give to the shoulders a liberty which one never thought they possessed

The employment of energy by the rider, when it is well applied, has also a moral effect on the horse, which hastens results. If the impulsion communicated by the legs finds in the hands the energy and tact necessary to regulate the effect, the pain which the horse feels will be always proportioned to his resistance, and his instinct will soon show him how to lessen it, and even to avoid it, by yielding promptly to his rider's demands. He will then hasten to submit himself and even to anticipate our desires. But, I repeat, it is only by tact, and lightness and discretion in the use of the spurs that one arrives at this important point. If the legs communicate a too great impulsion, the horse will very quickly overcome the action of the hands, and will regain with his natural position all the advantages which it gives to his bad Instincts to counteract the efforts of the rider. If, on the other hand, the hand offers a too strong resistance, the horse will soon force the legs, and will find by thus getting behind the legs a means of defence. These difficulties ought not! to disturb one too much; they are not really grave except when there is not any reasoned principle which enables one to overcome them. The properly carried out application of my method will enable the most ordinary horseman to obtain these results, which were looked upon as impossible of attainment up till now.

When the horse has become accustomed to this collection with the attacks of the spurs, it will become easy to overcome with the spurs all the resistances which can still manifest themselves. Since the movement from side to side, or the removal of the hindquarters from the centre are always the cause of these resistances, the spur by bringing the hind legs towards the middle of the body, will prevent the backward extension of the hocks, which would prevent the proper distribution of energy and weight.

This means is the one which I always use when bringing a horse to the halt from a fast gallop; without straining the hocks or other joints in the hindquarters. One understands that, since it is the hocks which drive the horse forward, it is sufficient to prevent them from extending themselves to stop the forward spring. The spur, by instantly bringing the hind legs under the body, immediately destroys their power, when the resistance of the hand fixes them in this position. The quarters then bend, the croup lowers itself, the weight and energy are distributed in the way most favourable to the free and combined play of every part, and the violence of the shock, thoroughly decomposed, is hardly felt by either the rider or the horse.

If, on the other hand, the rider stops his horse by using the hands before the legs, the hocks remain behind the body; the shock is violent, painful to the horse, and disastrous to his physical organisation. One should not commence the attacks of the spurs until the horse has been brought well in hand by the combined action of the legs and hands, and it is then that the rider will give the first touches of the spurs. It is essential when dealing with very irritable horses to wear spurs without sharp rowels, and not to use them unless the strongest pressure of the legs has not the desired effect; it is often useful with this kind of horse to give him a special education in the spur, that is to say, one should train him to answer freely to the spur by practising the attacks at first when standing, and then at the walk, without demanding anything more. This judicious employment of the spur gives immediate and lasting results; but, that the effect may be fruitful, it must bring about the proper balance of the horse. The rider will continue to make use of the spurs until the horse no longer offers any resistance to the hand, and avoids the pressure of the bit by bringing his chin in towards the chest. Once this submission has been attained, one can make use of the attacks of the spurs in cases of resistance, but the rider must be careful to discontinue them the moment the horse is light in hand. This means will have the double advantage of acting morally and physically. The first attacks will be made with one spur only, whilst stretching the rein on the other side to meet the Impulsion; these diagonal oppositions will have a more accurate effect and will give quicker results. When the horse commences to draw himself together In response to each spur used separately, the rider will be able to use them together and with an equal pressure.

To work then, Messieur horsemen ! If you will follow my instructions I can promise you that your purses will not empty themselves so often into the hands of horse dealers, and that you will make a pleasant mount of the worst of horses. You will even succeed in pleasing the directors of our horse breeding establishments, who will attribute to their attempts at regeneration the elegance and the grace which your art alone has given to your horses.

Riding with slack reins.—We now teach the horse to maintain a perfect balance without the assistance of the reins. The suppleness given to all parts of the horse., the accord between the aids of the hands and legs, teach him to carry himself in the best possible position. To know precisely if this result is attained, one should frequently slacken the reins, and this is how it is done; after having placed the right hand at the end of the reins and made certain that they arc of equal length, the rider removes the left hand and drops his right hand on to the pommel of the saddle. In order that this slackening of the reins may be regular the horse should neither increase nor decrease the speed of the pace, nor change the good position of his head and neck. At first, when thus left to himself, the horse will perhaps only take a few steps whilst preserving the same position and the same degree of speed: the rider should then first close in his legs, and then tighten the reins in order to replace the horse in his proper position: the frequent repetition of this exercise, after a horse has been perfectly balanced, will give him a finer contact with his rider, and the latter a much more delicate feeling with his horse. The means of direction employed by the rider will have a more immediate response if the energy of the horse is first distributed so as to produce a perfect harmony of his parts. The reins should be slackened in this way first at the walk, then at the trot, and lastly, at the gallop. This liberty gives such confidence to the horse that he unconsciously yields himself to his rider, and becomes his slave whilst thinking that he preserves his absolute independence.

Collection.—The preceding work will make it easy for the rider to collect his horse to the finest point of balance, which requires—

(1) The partial and general suppling of the neck and hindquarters.

(2) The perpendicular position of the head which results from the suppling exercises.

(3) The absorption by the rider, with the help of the spurs, of the whole energy of the horse.

Now, as the means of obtaining these different results have never been explained in any work on equitation, am I not right in saying that perfect collection has not been practised up till now? It is, nevertheless, one of the indispensable conditions of the horse's education: consequently, I have the same right to maintain that before my method was introduced no one had really trained horses whose conformation was defective. How, in fact, did they define collection in the Riding Schools? "One collects the horse by raising the hand and closing in the legs." I ask how would this movement help a rider mounted, on a horse at once badly formed, contracted, and under the control of all the evil propensities of his nature? This mechanical use of hands, far from making a horse obedient, cannot have any other effect than to increase his powers of resistance, since whilst warning him that we are going to demand a movement, we are powerless to distribute his energy so as to force him to obey, unless the horse's previous education has been conducted according to my method. *The true collection consists in gathering into the centre of the horse his whole energy, in order to lighten the two extremities and to place them completely under the control of the rider.* To explain this we will say that collection is shown by the hind legs being placed under the horse near the centre of his body, and we shall establish several degrees of collection indispensable to the ease and right performance of the different paces and the various high school movements. To thoroughly understand this the following diagram will be of assistance :—

Forehand	Centre	Hindquarters

7 6 5 4 3 2 1 0

I must again say, before commencing these effects of collection, that the horse must be perfectly in hand, and he must answer to the spurs by bringing himself together: it will then be easy to shorten, without painful constraint, the stride of the fore legs, and increase that of the hind legs. The first effect of collection which will bring the hind legs to the degrees 1, 2, 3, will be useful for the cadenced or extended trot, or the canter. This collection can be obtained at the walk by closing in the legs firmly and giving light touches of the spurs, whilst the hand confines itself to overcoming the contractions prejudicial to the balance. It is by this means that one causes the hind legs to increase their speed of movement. With regard to the more complete collection in which the hind legs reach the degrees 4, 5, 6, 7, it is necessary to stop the horse and increase the number of oppositions of the hands, legs, or spurs, until the horse mobilises himself as much as possible without advancing, or at any rate only advancing imperceptibly, he should then becalmed by a steady feeling with the hands and legs. The frequent repetition of this mobility, more or less regular, of the legs, will insensibly produce the most complete collection, which will give the "piaffer" with rhythm, measure and cadence. If the horse is well made the collection will be easily obtained, as also the- most complicated movements which depend upon it. It remains to be found out if it is possible to attempt them, when one's horse is badly made, that is to say, possesses some of the following faults—a low croup, or one that is too high in respect to the withers; small thighs; hocks too bent, placed too near to or too far from one another; too much or too little action. I am forced to acknowledge that these sorts of horses offer great difficulties, but by overcoming them one proves oneself not only a horseman, but also a man of intelligence and sense, with a right understanding of the horse.

I have already explained and proved that the horse has not a hard mouth, and I have said that the weakness of the loins, and the bad position of the hindquarters, were the only causes of the horse's resistance. In fact, if the length of the loins, for example, places the hind legs behind the position they ought to have to make the movement regular, the bending and extension of the hocks, which receive the weight and drive it forward again, can only be carried out with pain: to remedy these defects it is necessary to have recourse to the first degrees of collection, when once the horse has become light in hand; in this case the hind legs will come forward to the centre, and will be placed where they naturally would be in a well-shaped horse. In fact, why do certain horses resist with the neck and lower jaw? It is because the loins, the quarters and the hocks do not properly perform their work, and oppose themselves to the translation of weight which produces "the movement. This is proved by the fact that, the lighter a horse is in hand, and the more *naturally* mobile his lower jaw is, the nearer his conformation approaches to perfection. In such a horse the different parts of his body are so well placed and proportioned, that a perfect balance can be obtained immediately. Complete collection also, so easy to well-made horses, is a very great difficulty to a horse of poor conformation, because the effort which he makes to bring forward his hind legs takes so much from the movement necessary in the flexion which produces the elevation: furthermore this sort of horse offers great difficulties when one tries to get it to execute complicated precise work; it is certainly not impossible, but it is necessary to use methodical means, and to be endowed with much tact; I would even say that a similar task would fail, if it were undertaken by a rider who did not practise my method in all its details and thoroughness. The badly made horse, trained to do difficult work, is far from pleasing to the eye of people who are not interested in horsemanship, but how beautiful he is to those who have skill and knowledge ! The horseman has done better than nature.

The complete collection, that is a collection which brings the hind legs to the degrees of from 4 to 7, serves for the "piaffer"; the cadenced trot called the passage; the slow animated canter; the pirouettes on the hindquarters, etc. It is indispensable in all the elevated movements, because, in the complete collection, the hocks execute more easily the upward than the forward flexion, which proves that once the complete collection has been obtained, the horse can execute the most difficult movements without feeling any pain, and without injury; his position is always right and his movements graceful.

The horse then finds himself transformed, so to speak, into a pair of scales, of which the rider is the needle. The least additional weight placed upon one or other of the extremities, which represent the scales, immediately inclines them in the desired direction.

The rider will know that the collection is complete when he feels his horse, so to speak, ready to spring from all four legs. It is with this work that we *give* a horse brilliance, and a graceful majestic carriage; he is no longer the same horse, the transformation is complete. Although we have been forced to employ the spur at first to bring to the utmost limit this concentration of energy, the legs will afterwards suffice to obtain the collection necessary for the cadence and elevation of all complicated movements.

Is it necessary for me to recommend discretion in the demands made on the horse? Certainly not; if the rider, after having reached this point in the education of his horse, does not understand, and make himself master of the fineness of tact, and the nicety of procedure, indispensable to the proper application of these principles, it will be a proof that he has not the sentiment of horsemanship, and I cannot remedy this defect of his nature.

CHAPTER VII

THE CANTER—JUMPING—THE PIAFFER

The Canter.—Up till now the greater part of the resources of horsemanship have not been understood, and if I had need of a new proof in support of my opinion, I could find it in the errors, superstitions, and numberless contradictions, which have been piled up to explain the simple movement of the canter. What disagreement there is, for instance, as to the means that [should be employed to start a horse on the off fore leg ! Some say that it is the pressure of the rider's right leg I which determines the movement; others maintain |that it is the left leg; whilst others recommend the equal pressure of both legs. How can one arrive at the | truth in the midst of this conflict of principles so contrary to one another? We know that the contraction of any part of the horse always reacts on the neck, and that the stiffness of the neck prevents the proper | execution of every movement. Now, if, at the moment he raises himself for the canter the horse contracts one of his extremities, and consequently his neck, what use is there in my demanding, in order to start the horse into a canter leading with the off fore leg, that the rider should close in one or other leg, or even both legs together? These means would evidently be without effect until I have dealt with the cause of the resistance and overcome it. One therefore sees in this case, as in all others, that suppleness and lightness in hand arc alone able to render the execution of work easy. If, when one wishes to start the horse on the off fore leg, a slight contraction of a part of the horse disposes him to start on the near fore leg, and if one persists, notwithstanding this bad Inclination, in forcing the horse to start on the off fore leg, It will. be necessary to use the lateral aids, *i.e.* the left leg and left hand; the first to start the movement and the second to overcome the opposition of the horse.

But when the horse, perfectly supple and collected, only moves the different parts of his body in accordance with the directions his rider gives, the latter, In order. to start the horse on the off fore leg, should combine his aids so as to keep the horse balanced, whilst at the same time placing him in the position proper for the movement. He will, therefore, carry the hand to the left and close in the right leg. One sees from this that the means, of which I have made mention, useful when the horse is not properly placed, would be prejudicial when the horse is in the right position, since they will destroy the harmony which exists between the different parts of the body.

This short explanation will, I hope, suffice to make it clear that one should thoroughly study a subject before forming principles. Let us, therefore, hear no] more about the employment of one or the other leg to start the canter: my firm conviction Is that the first condition of this movement, and, in fact, of any movement, Is to keep the horse supple and light in hand, that Is to say, in the state of collection necessary for the pace; It will be easy to appreciate the degree of collection by the lightness in hand, and the ease with which the weight of the forehand is carried back to the hindquarters; then one will use one or the other leg according as, at the start, the horse preserves his proper position, or tries to leave it. One must also bear in mind that it is the aids which give the horse the position, and that the regularity of the movement depends entirely on the position.

The frequent change, on the straight line and with half halts, from the canter on the right leg to that on the left leg, will soon enable the horse to change every step. We must be careful to avoid violent applications of the aids, which would only confuse the horse and destroy the lightness in hand. We should remember that this lightness in hand, which should precede all the changes of pace or direction, and which makes easy, graceful, and inevitable all movements, is the important condition to which we should devote our greatest attention.

It is because they have not understood this principle, and have not realised that the first condition for preparing a horse for the canter is to overcome all the instinctive resistances to the position necessary for the movement, that instructors in horsemanship have laid down on this subject so many false principles, and that not one of them has been able to indicate the right means to employ.

Jumping.—Although the science of horsemanship cannot give to every horse the energy and vigour necessary for jumping, there are, nevertheless, principles by the aid of which one will succeed in supplementing to some extent the natural aptitude of the horse. The rider will assist the height and freedom of the spring by giving a good direction to the energy. I do not pretend to say by this that an indifferently made horse will jump as high or in as good form as a well-made one, but he will be at least able to make the utmost use of such physical qualities as he possesses.

The principal point is to get the horse to jump kindly. If the rider carefully follows out the instructions I have given for overcoming the instinctive resistances of the horse, he will realise the use of this progression in training by the ease with which he can get his horse to jump anything he comes across. Moreover, he should never, when the horse refuses, have recourse to strong means of persuasion, such as the lunging whip, nor try to excite the horse by shouting at him, which will only have a terrifying effect. It is by physical means above all others that we should bring him to obedience, as they alone will enable him to understand what is wanted, and to jump. The rider should, therefore, remain calm, and try to overcome the energy which the horse exerts in refusing, by getting it into his own control: he should wait, before asking a horse to jump, till he answers freely to the legs and spurs, so as always to have a certain means of domination.

The bar should be on the ground until the horse passes over it • without hesitation; and it should be gradually raised until it is at a height which the horse can jump without much exertion. To go beyond this would risk giving the horse a dislike for jumping, which must be carefully avoided. The bar thus carefully raised should be fixed, so that the horse,, if he happens to be lazy, may not play with an obstacle, which becomes no longer serious the moment it is knocked over by a mere touch of his legs. The bar should not be covered with anything soft, as one should be severe when the demands are not excessive, and one should avoid the disorder which is always encouraged by misplaced kindness.

Before putting his horse at a jump, the rider should fix himself in the saddle with sufficient firmness to prevent his body preceding the movement of the horse. His loins should be supple, and his seat bones pressed well into the saddle, so that he will not feel any shock or violent reaction. His thighs and his legs enveloping the horse's body will give him an opportune and infallible strength of seat. His hand in its natural position will stretch the reins sufficiently to feel the mouth of the horse, and so be able to judge the effect of the impulsion given by the legs. In this position the rider will take his horse up to the jump, and if the latter arrives at it with plenty of energy in his pace, a light opposition of the hands and legs will raise the forehand, and give the necessary driving power to the hindquarters. The moment the horse rises, the hand teases its effect, and feels the mouth again when the fore legs again come to the ground and prevents them from giving under the weight of the body.

The rider should be contented with a few jumps according to the capability of his horse, and he should never over-mark him. I have known good jumpers which have been completely ruined by this, and which could not be made to jump places half the size of those which before they cleared with the greatest case and confidence.

The "piaffer."—Owing to the training we have given the horse, we can now collect all his energy in the centre of his body, and bring his hind legs also almost to this point: the horse which can be collected to this extent is capable of executing the piaffer, and all other high school movements, such as changing the leading leg in the canter every two strides and every stride. In order that the "piaffer" may be regular and graceful it is necessary that the diagonal legs of the horse rise and fall together with as long a time of suspension between the steps as possible The horse should be as light to the hand as to the leg, and be in perfect balance. When the energy is thus gathered into the centre of the body and the collection is perfect, it is sufficient, in order to commence the "piaffer," to communicate to the horse with the legs a light and frequent, vibration, arousing an energy which is under the absolute control of the rider.

On this first result being obtained, the rider should start the horse in the walk, and closing in his legs gradually, he should slightly increase his action, then, but then only, the hand should strengthen its action in accord with that of the legs, and at the same intervals, so that the two aids acting together excite a succession of imperceptible movements, and produce a light contraction, which spreads over the whole body of the horse, and gives to the legs a mobility which at first will be far from regular. The rider should be contented during the first few days of training with the mere mobility of the legs, and should stop his horse every time he raises and puts down his feet without advancing, pat him and speak kindly to him, and so calm the excitement caused by a demand he does not yet understand. These caresses should be given with discretion and when the horse has made a true step, otherwise they will be harmful: yielding the legs and hands at the right moment is still more important, and to this the rider must devote much attention. When once the mobility of the legs has been obtained the rider can commence to regulate and cadence the steps. Here again I find it impossible to explain in writing the nicety which is necessary in the application of the aids, since their effects must be produced with perfect justice and at exactly the right moment. It is by the alternate touch of the two legs that the rider will succeed in prolonging the lateral poise of the horse's body, so as to keep it longer on one side or the other. The rider will take advantage of the moment when the horse is about to place a fore foot on the ground, to close in the leg of the same side, and so increase the inclination of the horse's body in the same direction. This action of the legs is very difficult and requires a lot of practice; but the results are so brilliant that the trouble which brings proficiency is well repaid,

CHAPTER VIII

SCHEME OF WORK

I have explained my method of educating the horse, and the principles which, if properly carried out, should quickly bring him under the control of the rider, make him graceful and true in. his movement; increase his strength and develop his intellect. I pride myself on having said much in few words, and I have only dealt with the effects in order to explain their cause, avoiding a multitude of minute details which do but reduce great and beautiful truths to very pleasing little nothings. It now remains for me to explain how the trainer should arrange his work, so as to connect the different exercises and to pass gradually from the simple to the complex. Two months' work, of two lessons of half an hour each a day, *i.e.* twenty lessons, will amply suffice to teach the greenest horse to carry out with regularity all the exercises which I have recommended. I believe in giving two short lessons each day, one in the morning and the other in the afternoon; as I think in this way one gets the best results.

You sicken a young horse by keeping him too long at tiring exercises, all the more because his intelligence is not sufficiently developed to understand what is wanted. Moreover, an interval of twenty-four hours is too long, according to my idea, for the horse to easily remember his previous lesson. The general work should be divided into five lessons arranged *in* the following order.

First lesson. Eight days' work.—The first twenty minutes of this lesson should be given up to flexions of the lower jaw and neck, the horse being at the halt and the trainer on foot at first and then mounted. During the last ten minutes he should walk the horse, and give his whole attention to keeping the head perpendicular with the ground and the lower jaw relaxed. He should be content with one change of hand, so that the horse has equal practice to both hands. On the fourth or fifth day the rider, before putting his horse in movement, should gently move the quarters from side to side.

Second lesson. Ten days' work.—The first fifteen minutes should be given up to flexions at the halt, including movements of the hindquarters to a greater extent than in the first lesson; the rider will then commence to teach the rein-back. The rest of the lesson should be given up to walking in a straight line, varied by short slow trots. The rider, during this second part of the work, whilst keeping the head and neck in their proper position, should lightly oppose the hands to the action of the legs, so as to prepare the horse for their simultaneous action, and to give regularity to the paces. One should also commence the changes of direction at the walk, keeping the head perpendicular and the horse light in hand, and being careful to turn the head and neck to the desired direction before using the legs.

Third lesson. Twelve days' work.—Only six or eight minutes should be devoted to stationary flexions: those of the hindquarters being carried out till they make a complete circle round the forehand. One should then give a lesson in the rein-back, and devote the rest of the time to making perfect the walk and the trot, and in this latter pace commencing the changes of direction. The rider should often halt his horse, and should pay careful attention to keeping the head perpendicular and the lower jaw relaxed during the changes of pace and direction. He should commence I to teach the movement on two lines in the walk, and also the rotation of the shoulders round the quarters.

Fourth lesson. Fifteen days' work.—After devoting; five minutes to the stationary flexions, the rider should first repeat the third lesson; and then commence, at the halt, the spur attacks in order to confirm the lightness in hand, and prepare the horse for collection. He should repeat the spur attacks at the walk, and when the horse becomes accustomed to them he should start the canter. At first he should be satisfied with four or five strides, and then put the horse back into the walk and restart the canter on the other *leg*, unless the particular horse requires more training on one *leg* than the other. In changing from the trot to the walk, one should take care that the horse takes this latter pace quickly, and without jogging, and with the head perpendicular and the lower jaw relaxed. The rider should only exercise his horse in the canter at the end of each lesson.

Fifth lesson. Fifteen days' work.—These last fifteen days should be employed in making perfect all the previous work, and in giving the final instruction in the canter, until the horse easily changes his direction, changes his leading leg at every stride, and works on two lines. One should then give lessons in jumping and in the "piaffer." Thus in two months with no matter what horse, we shall have accomplished a task which formerly required years, and even then gave but incomplete results, Finally, I repeat that however insufficient so short a time may seem, it will produce the effect that I have promised, if one conforms exactly to all my instructions. I have proved it in hundreds of cases, and many of my pupils have had the same success. Whilst laying down this order for the work, it should be understood that I am dealing with horses in general. A trainer with any tact will quickly find out what modifications he should apply, according to the special nature of his pupil. One horse, for example, will require more training in the flexions: another in the rein-back; another without fire and sluggish will require the spur attacks at an earlier stage of his training than • I have recommended. All this is an affair of intelligence, and I should be insulting my readers if I did not think them capable of adding to the details what it is impossible to lay down with precision. One can easily understand that there are irritable, badly formed horses, spoilt perhaps in their early training, which will require longer work at the flexions and at the walk, but notwithstanding this, two months should still be sufficient to produce the energy and aptitude necessary for all the movements, though the *finishing* of the education in this time will depend upon the tact and precision of the rider.

CHAPTER IX

A CONCISE EXPLANATION OF THE METHOD BY MEANS OF QUESTION AND ANSWER

Q. What do you mean by energy ?

A. The motive power which results from muscular contraction.

Q. What do you mean by instinctive energy ?

A. The energy which a horse uses on his own initiative.

Q. What do you mean by transmitted energy ?

A. Energy aroused and controlled by the rider.

Q. What do you mean by resistances ?

A. The energy which a horse uses to get the better of his rider.

Q. Should one first overcome the resistances before demanding other movements ?

A. Certainly, because in this case the rider's energy intended to displace the weight of the horse's body is absorbed by a resistance of equal force, and all movement becomes impossible.

Q. By what means can we overcome resistances ?

A. By the methodical suppling of the lower jaw, the neck, the quarters and the loins.

Q. What is the use of suppling the lower jaw ?

A. Since the effects of the rider's hands in the first place influence the lower jaw, these effects would be incomplete if the lower jaw is contracted, or tightly closed against the upper jaw. Moreover, as in this case the displacements of the horse's body can only be obtained with difficulty, the resulting movements will also be awkward.

Q. Is it sufficient that the horse tastes the bit to make the flexion of the lower jaw perfect ?

A. No, the horse must also yield to the bit, that is, he must open the two jaws to the full extent.

Q. Can all horses have this suppleness of lower jaw ?

A. All without exception, if one follows the method recommended, and if the rider does not allow himself to be deceived by the flexion of the neck. Although this flexion is useful, it is insufficient without the mobility of the lower jaw.

Q. In the direct flexion of the lower jaw should one stretch both the bridoon and the bit reins ?

A. No, one should first use the bridoon reins until the head and neck are lowered and then the pressure of the bit, in accord with that of the bridoon, will promptly cause the jaws to open.

Q. Should one repeat this exercise often ?

A. One should continue it until the jaws open on the slightest pressure of the bit or bridoon.

Q. Why is the stiffness of the neck an equally powerful obstacle to the education of the horse ?

A. Because it makes its own use of the energy which the rider is trying to distribute over the body.

Q. Can the hindquarters be suppled by themselves ?

A. Yes, certainly, and this exercise is comprised in what Is called stationary work.

Q. What Is the use of it ?

A. To anticipate the bad effects resulting from the Instinctive use of energy by the horse, and to make him willingly carry out the wishes of the rider with the energy which he has aroused,

Q. Can a horse execute a movement without transferring weight ?

A. This is Impossible: one must try to make the horse take a position which will so affect his balance., that the movement becomes a natural consequence.

Q. What do you mean by position ?

A. The placing of the head and neck of the horse in the right position for the movement desired.

Q. In what does the "Rammener" consist ?

A. In the perpendicular position of the head, in the mobility of the lower jaw, and in the lightness and balance which is the result.

Q. What is the distribution of energy and weight In the balanced position ?

A. The energy and the weight are equally distributed over the whole body.

Q. How does one appeal to the horse's intelligence ?

A. By the position one gives him; in the sense that it is the position which explains to the horse the intentions of the rider.

Q. Why is it that in the "rein-back" the action of the rider's legs precedes that of his hands ?

A. Because he must first displace the base before putting on it the weight it should carry.

Q. Should the rider force the horse to do anything ?

A. No, the rider speaks to the horse by arousing his energy and giving him a position; and the horse replies by the change of pace or direction which the rider asks for.

Q, Should one attribute a bad bit of work to the rider or to the horse ?

A. To the rider always, because it is his work to supple and place the horse properly for the movement, and when these two conditions are faithfully fulfilled everything becomes regular; the rider, therefore, deserves all the praise or blame.

Q. What kind of bit suits a horse ?

A. The mild bit.

Q. Why should one use a mild bit with all horses, no matter what resistance they may offer ?

A. Because the severe bit always contracts and surprises the horse, whereas one should prevent him from doing wrong, and enable him to do right. Now one can only obtain these results with the assistance of a mild bit and a trained hand, because the bit is the hand, and a good hand is everything in horsemanship.

Q. Are there any other bad results from the use of instruments of torture called strong bits ?

A. Certainly, the horse soon learns to avoid the painful restraint by forcing the rider's legs, whose power can never be equal to that of a cruel bit. The horse gains the victory by yielding his body and resisting with his neck and mouth, which defeats the end aimed at.

Q, How is it that nearly all well-known horsemen have invented bits to which they attribute marvellous effects ?

A. Because being without any personal talent they try to make good their deficiency by mechanical means.

Q. Can a horse who is perfectly balanced resist ?

A. No; because the proper distribution of weight which gives this position, produces a perfect regularity in the movements, and all this must be changed before the horse can rebel.

Q. What is the use of the bridoon ?

A. The bridoon overcomes the opposition of the neck, it causes the head to lead all changes of direction when the horse is not yet used to the bit; it also keeps the head and neck in a perfectly straight line.

Q. Should the legs and hands act separately, or ought they to assist one another ?

A. Each of these aids should be assisted by the other.

Q. Should one keep the horse for a long time at the same pace to develop his strength ?

A. This is useless, since the regularity of the movement results from the regularity of the positions, the horse which trots fifty steps regularly is much farther advanced in his education than if he trotted a thousand steps in a bad position. It is, therefore, to the position that one must pay attention, that is, to the lightness in hand.

Q. To what extent should one use the horse's energy ?

A. This cannot be defined, as energy varies in different horses, but one should be careful and circumspect in its use, especially during the course of education; it is necessary, so to speaks to create a reservoir and not allow the horse to exhaust his energy uselessly; by this means the rider will make his horse last many years.

Q. How will the horse benefit from this judicious use of his energy ?

A. As one will only make use of the energy necessary for the movement, fatigue or exhaustion will only result from keeping the horse too long at a fast pace, and not from the effect, even at the slow paces, of maintaining an excessive and useless contraction of the muscles.

Q. When should one try to obtain the first backward steps from the horse ?

A. After suppling the neck and quarters, and after having obtained a perfect lightness in hand.

Q. Why should the suppling of the quarters precede that of the loins (the rein-back) ?

A. To more easily keep the horse on a straight line and make easy the backward and forward movement of weight.

Q. Should these lessons in the "rein-back" be prolonged at first ?

A. No, since their aim is to gain control of the horse's energy, it is necessary to wait until he is perfectly in hand before we can get the true "rein-back."

Q. What constitutes the true "rein-back," and how is it obtained ?

A. By a gradual pressure of the legs, which puts the horse in motion and causes him to raise one of the hind legs as if to move forwards; the hand will then, by increasing the tension on the reins, force the raised leg to move backwards. When one has obtained a first step the. hand should be eased, in order that the weight, which has to be carried back, may, by coming forward, enable the horse to again raise a leg, and the hand again to make him move it to the rear.

Q. How close to the sides should the spurs be before an attack ?

A. The rowel should not be more than 1½ to 2 inches from the sides of the horse.

Q. How should the attacks be given ?

A. The spurs should strike the sides like the stab of a lancet and be immediately withdrawn.

Q. Should the attack ever be made without the support of the hand ?

A. Never, because their only use is to arouse the energy which enables the hand to collect the horse.

Q. Do the attacks in themselves punish the horse ?

A. No; the punishment is in their tying a horse up between the hand and the spurs, and so making it impossible for him to use his energy in opposition to his rider,

Q. What is the difference between the attacks as practised according to the old teaching, and those which the new method prescribes ?

A. Under the old method the spurs were used to drive the horse beyond himself; under my method they draw his ends together, and thus give him the position which is the mother of all others.

Q. What is the *rôle* of the legs during the attacks ?

A. The legs should remain closed into the sides, and should not accompany the movements of the feet.

Q. When should one commence the attacks ?

A. When the horse quietly supports the pressure of the legs without getting out of hand.

Q. Why does a horse, well in hand, take the spur without excitement or sudden movements ?

A. Because the skilfulness of the rider's hand, having prevented any movement of the head, never lets any of the energy escape, but concentrates and fixes it: the equal distribution of energy amongst the opposing parts sufficiently explains the apparent calmness of the horse.

Q. Is there not ground for fear that these attacks may make the horse insensible to the leg, and that the rider will not have the means of arousing his energy for the fast paces ?

A. Although this opinion is held by nearly all those who talk about my method without understanding it, there is not anything in it. Since my method merely keeps the horse in the most perfect balance, quickness of movement must of necessity result, and consequently the horse will be disposed to answer to the progressive pressure of the legs, when the hand does not oppose their action.

Q. How does one know when the attack is regular ?

A. When instead of making the horse get out of hand it brings him into it.

Q. How should the hand act when the horse resists ?

A. The hand should steady and fix itself and bring itself only so far back as to give the reins a three-quarter tension, and wait till the horse is driven against the bit.

Q. What would be the bad result of increasing the pressure of the bit by bringing the hand back to the body to stop the horse or to get him in hand. ?

A. It would act on the whole of the horse's energy, and

instead of producing the partial effect of displacing weight it would overwhelm the force of impulsion. One should not try to overturn that which one cannot stop.

Q. Under what circumstances should one make use of the cavesson, and with what purpose ?

A. One should use it when the bad conformation of the horse makes him resist, even when asked to execute simple movements. It is also advisable to use the cavesson with restive horses, and it should influence the moral of the horse, whilst the rider maintains a physical control.

Q. How should one use the cavesson ?

A. One should at first hold it close to the horse's head with a firm hand, and seize the right moment to diminish or increase the pressure of the cavesson on the horse's nose, using it in fact as an aid. Every disorderly movement should be repressed by slight jerks at the moment the horse commences to go wrong. As soon as the movements of the rider commence to be understood by the horse, the cavesson should cease its action, and after a few days there will not be any further use for it, and the horse will answer readily to the bit alone.

Q. When is the rider less intelligent than the horse ?

A. When the horse is the master.

Q. Are the resistances of the horse physical or moral ?

A. The resistances are at first physical and they subsequently become moral; the rider should, therefore, find out their cause and try by preparatory exercises to re-establish the proper balance which an evil disposition had refused to take.

Q. Can a horse, naturally well-balanced, resist his rider ?

A. It is just as difficult for a really well-made horse to give himself up to disorderly movements, as it is impossible for a badly made horse to have regular movements without the assistance of skilful training.

Q. What do you mean by collection ?

A. The bringing of the hind legs under the centre of the body combined with perfect lightness in hand.

Q. Can one collect a horse which cannot be brought together by the spur attacks ?

A. It is absolutely impossible; the legs would not be able to counterbalance the effects of the hand.

Q. When should one commence to collect a horse ?

A. When the head and neck are thoroughly supple and obedient.

Q. What is the use of collection ?

A. To obtain with ease all that is complicated in horsemanship.

Q. What is the "piaffer"?

A. The graceful pose of the horse's body, and the harmonised cadence of the legs.

Q. Are there many kinds of "piaffer"?

A. Two, the slow and the hurried.

Q. Of the two which is preferable ?

A. The slow "piaffer," as it is only when this is obtained that the balance is perfect.

Q. Should one make a horse "piaffer" which will not support collection ?

A. No. It would be a reversal of the logical sequence of training which alone gives good results.

Q. Are all horsemen capable of overcoming all the difficulties, and of availing themselves of all the effects of tact ?

A. As all the results of equitation are based upon intelligence, everything depends upon the possession of it;

but all horsemen will be able to train their horses, if they confine the education of the horse within the bounds of his individual capacity.

Made in the USA
Columbia, SC
06 January 2019